James Breckinridge Waller

The True Doctrine of State Rights

With an Examination of the Record of the Democratic and Republican

Parties in Connection with Slavery

James Breckinridge Waller

The True Doctrine of State Rights
With an Examination of the Record of the Democratic and Republican Parties in Connection with Slavery

ISBN/EAN: 9783744733717

Printed in Europe, USA, Canada, Australia, Japan

Cover: Foto ©ninafisch / pixelio.de

More available books at **www.hansebooks.com**

The True Doctrine

OF

STATE RIGHTS

WITH

AN EXAMINATION OF THE RECORD

OF

The Democratic and Republican Parties

IN CONNECTION WITH

SLAVERY.

By JAMES B. WALLER.

CHICAGO.
JAMESON & MORSE, PRINTERS, 162-4 SOUTH CLARK STREET.
1880.

TO do justice to our subject, it is first necessary to bring prominently before us the distinguished parts taken by Jefferson and Madison in laying the foundations of our government, and in its practical administration.

They were the founders and fathers of it. One the author of the Declaration of Independence, which gave birth to us as a nation, and proclaimed to the world those great truths which lie at the foundation of all just governments — truths which were not intended to define the individual rights of men in their personal or social relations to each other, so much as of communities of people in uniting together to establish sovereign states, or independent political organizations, for the government of themselves and their posterity. Such were the thirteen Colonies of Great Britain, when they met together on the 4th of July, 1776, and such the rights which they proclaimed to belong equally to all men in the construction of their own governments. To use the very language of the Declaration, it declared "That all men are created equal; that they are endowed with certain unalienable rights ; that among them are life, liberty, and the pursuit of happiness. That to secure these rights governments are instituted among men, deriving their just powers from the consent of the governed; that whenever any form of government becomes destructive of those ends, it is the right of the people to alter or abolish it, and to institute a new government." This was the masterly statement of our rights, drawn by the hand of Jefferson himself, which not only justified the Colonies in their act of separation, but guided them afterwards in the formation of their government.

On the 11th of June, 1776, a committee of one delegate from each state had been appointed to prepare Articles of Confederation between the states, which articles, on the 12th of July, 1776, were reported to Congress, and approved by that body on the 15th of November, 1777, and afterwards, at different times, ratified by each of the State Legislatures. This constitution was not satisfactory to Mr. Jefferson, who, during its pendency for adoption. first suggested the principles on which the Senate and House of Representatives are at present organized. Mr. Bancroft says, " 'The vote,' said Sherman, of Connecticut, 'should be taken two ways; call the Colonies, and call the individuals, and have a majority of both.' This idea he probably derived from Jefferson, who enforced in private as a means to save the Union, that any proposition might be negatived by the Representatives of a majority of the people, or of a majority of the Colonies. Here is the thought out of which the great compromise of our constitution was evolved." Mr. Jefferson was Governor of Virginia from 1779 to 1781. In 1784 he was appointed by Congress minister to France, where he remained as such for five years. He returned in 1789, when Washington appointed him Secretary of State, which office he resigned in 1793.

His great friend and cotemporary, James Madison, graduated at Princeton, New Jersey, in 1772, was a member of the Convention of Virginia which formed her first constitution in 1776: was a member of her Legislature till 1777; and from 1780 until 1789, was in the Congress of the Confederacy; afterwards, from 1784 to 1786, he was again a member of the Virginia Legislature. In 1786 a proposition was made by Mr. Madison, and adopted by the Annapolis Convention, to call a general convention of all the states to assemble at Philadelphia in May, of the following year, for changing the Articles of Confederation; which accordingly assembled and formed our present constitution. In view of such a convention, Mr. Jefferson in 1786 wrote a letter to Mr. Madison from France, in which he proposed the great and radical amendment to the then Federal Constitution which was most needed, and which distinguishes our present one from any Federal System of Government which ever preceeded it. In that letter Mr. Jefferson says: "To make us one nation as to foreign concerns, and keep us distinct in domestic ones, gives the outline of the proper division of powers between the general and particular government. But to enable the Federal head to exercise the power given it to the best advantage, it should be organized, as the particular ones are, into Legislative, Executive and Judiciary." The convention at Annapolis referred to was composed of commissioners from five states, and met on the 11th of September 1786. They adopted a report which was sent as a circular to the legislatures they represented, in which they advised the calling a general convention of all the states, to meet in Philadelphia, May, 1787, "to take into consideration the situation of the United States, to advise such further provisions as shall appear to them necessary to render the Constitution of the Federal Government adequate to the exigencies of the Union." That convention met on the 14th of May, 1787. Mr. Madison was a member of it. Determined as he said, "to preserve as far as could be an exact account of what might pass in the convention while executing its trust, I chose a seat in front of the presiding member, with the other members on my right and left hands. In this favorable position for hearing all that passed, I noted in terms legible, and in abbreviations and marks intelligible to myself, what was read from the chair, and spoken by members; and losing not a moment unnecessarily between the adjournment and reassembling of the convention, I was enabled to write out my daily notes during the session, or within a few finishing hours after its close. It happened also that I was not absent a single day, nor more than a casual fraction of an hour in any day, so that I could not have lost a single speech, unless a very short one." His papers, for which Congress since his death gave $30,000, contained the only extant copies of the debate, in this convention. He was also, as the proceedings show, by far the most active and efficient of its members, taking a leading part in all its most important measures; so much so, that he has been styled ever since "the Father of the Constitution." After the formation of the Constitution, he united with Hamilton and Jay in writing the work called the "Federalist," which ever since its publication has been held by American jurists and statesmen as a text book, and as the highest authority for a true exposition of the constitution. On account of his able defense of the then new constitution against a most powerful opposition, it was ratified by Virginia. After its adoption by the states, he became a member of the first Congress and successive ones; in which he served from 1789 to 1797.

The foregoing brief sketch of the political careers of Jefferson and Madison up to the closing period of the last century, has been given not to inform the public of facts so familiar to it, but to refresh the recollection of them, in order that the opinions, referred to hereafter, of those who were so pre-eminently the authors and earliest expounders of the constitution, may have their due weight in its construction. They, indeed, may be truly called, in comparison with all others in that age of heroes, the authors of two of the greatest productions of human genius ever made for the exposition of political liberty and for the security of human rights, the Declaration of American Independence, and the constitution of the United States.

At the close of the last century, during the administration of John Adams, a question of fearful import arose, as to the true construction of the constitution, which convulsed the Republic from centre to circumference, and which, although settled in 1800, and for many years thereafter, was again revived, and has continued ever since a source of agitation and angry controversy. Out of that question sprang the doctrine of "State Rights." In their names, through declarations made by Jefferson and Madison in that celebrated conflict, were proclaimed the true principles of the government of which they themselves were the great architects.

Let us now look into the nature of that conflict, and of the doctrine alluded to. During the administration of John Adams, the notorious alien and sedition laws were passed. The alien act provided, in substance, that the President should have power to order all aliens in the United States, whom he in his discretion thought dangerous to the peace and safety of the nation, to depart from the country. In regard to such aliens, he was invested with the exercise of legislative, judicial, and executive power. The sedition act was hostile to the freedom of the press, and its principle was to shield the President, and Congress, and officers of the government, against an unrestrained and unfettered criticism of their official acts. On the passage of these laws, Jefferson denounced them as palpable violations of the constitution, and as usurpations of power, dangerous to the rights of the states and to the liberties of the people. Through his instrumentality, appeals were made to the different state governments to take action against them; and to this end the famous Virginia and Kentucky resolutions of 1798 and '99, denouncing them, were passed; followed by the celebrated report of Mr. Madison.

The Virginia resolutions use the following language: "That this Assembly doth explicitly and peremptorily declare, that it views the powers of the Federal Government as resulting from the compact to which the states are parties, as limited by the plain sense and intention of the instrument constituting that compact, and that in case of a deliberate, palpable, and dangerous exercise of other powers not granted by the said compact, states who are parties thereto, have the right, and are in duty bound, to interpose for arresting the progress of the evil, and for maintaining, within their respective limits, the authorities, rights, and liberties appertaining to them."

"That the General Assembly doth also express its deep regret, that a spirit has, in sundry instances, been manifested by the Federal Government to enlarge its powers by a forced construction of the constitutional charter which defines them; and that indications have appeared of a design to expound certain general phrases (which having been copied from the very limited grant of powers in the former Articles of Confederation, were the less liable to be misconstrued) so as to destroy the meaning and effect of the particular enumeration which necessarily explains and limits the general phrases, and so as to consolidate the states by degrees into one sovereignty; the obvious tendency and inevitable result of which would be to transform the present republican system of the United States into an absolute, or, at best, mixed monarchy."

"That the good people of this Commonwealth having ever felt, and continuing to feel, the most sincere affection for their brethren of the other states, the truest anxiety for establishing and perpetuating the union of all, and the most scrupulous fidelity to that constitution which is the pledge of mutual friendship and the instrument of mutual happiness; the General Assembly doth solemnly appeal to the like disposition in the other states, in confidence that they will concur with this Commonwealth, in declaring, as it does hereby declare, that the acts aforesaid are unconstitutional; and that the necessary and proper measures will be taken by each for co-operating with this state in maintaining unimpaired the authorities, rights, and liberties reserved to the states respectively, or to the people."

"That the General Assembly doth particularly protest against the palpable and alarming infractions of the constitution in the two late cases of the Alien and Sedition Acts, passed at the last session of Congress."

Mr. Madison, in his celebrated report sustaining these resolutions, declares: "That the judicial department is, in all questions submitted to it by the forms of the constitution, to decide in the last resort; this resort must necessarily be deemed the last in relation to the authorities of the other departments of the government; not in relation to the rights of the parties to the constitutional compact, from which the judicial, as well as the other departments, hold their delegated trusts."

In these extracts are to be found those great conservative principles of our Government which have rendered these resolutions and report so illustrious, and almost as famous as the constitution itself.

In order to avoid a misconstruction of the positions taken in the above resolutions and report, and the reasoning used in both to sustain them, it must be remembered that the question raised by the Alien and Sedition laws was one between the general government and the states, as composing its constituent body. They gave rise also to another question, viz., how far a decision of the Supreme Court of the United States was a bar to the interposition of the states; it having been alleged to be so, even to the *declaration of legislative opinions*. The replies, at that time, to those resolutions from other states, indicate such a position as the latter to have been held. Massachusetts, in her reply, said: "They cannot admit *the right* of the State Legislatures to *denounce the administration* of that government to which the people themselves, by a solemn *compact*, have exclusively entrusted their national concerns;" "That the construction of all laws, made in pursuance of the constitution, is *exclusively* vested by the people in the judicial courts." Another conclusive proof that such a position was maintained, is the fact that, when the report of Mr. Madison was under consideration in the Virginia House of Delegates, a resolution was moved which affirms: "That protests made by the legislature of this, or any other state, against particular acts of Congress as unconstitutional, accompanied by invitations to other states to join in such protests, are improper and unauthorized assumptions of power, not permitted, nor intended to be permitted, to the state legislatures. And inasmuch as *correspondent sentiments* with the present have been expressed by those of our sister states who have acted on the resolutions (of 1798); Resolved, therefore, that the present General Assembly, convinced of the impropriety of the resolutions of the last Assembly, deem it inexpedient further to act on the said resolutions." Fifty-seven voted for, and ninety-eight against the passage of this dissent from the majority. Besides the above documentary evidence, Mr. Madison, in 1835, in commenting on his report and the proceedings of Virginia, makes the assertion, "That the right in the states to interpose *declarations and protests* against unconstitutional acts by Congress had been denied; and that the reasoning in the resolutions was *called for by that denial.*"

It will be observed that great care is taken, in the commencement of these proceedings, to proclaim the constitution to be a compact to which the states are parties. On this broad truth is established the Democratic doctrine of state rights and of strict construction. On the theory that it is not a compact between the states, but a constitution, in a different sense, formed "by the people in the aggregate," rests the doctrine of centralization. Mr. Webster, the greatest champion of this theory, declared it when opposing a doctrine equally false, he declares in these celebrated words: "The constitution of the United States is not a confederacy, or compact, between the people of the several states in their sovereign power. The constitution itself, in its very front, declares that it is ordained and established by the people of the United States. So far from saying that it is established by the governments of the several states, it does not even say that it is established by the people of the several states, but pronounces that it is established by the people in the aggregate."

To this it may be replied, that in the original draft of the constitution, after all its provisions had been adopted, the preamble instead of saying, "We, the people of the United States," specified each state by name, as the previous articles of confederation had done. During all the debates the preamble remained in this form in the front without objection. The constitution, *thus agreed to*, was then referred to a "Committee on Style," for verbal supervision and correction. By this committee the names of the states were omitted, and the clause made to read as at present, for the obvious reason that in its original form it became *irreconcilable* with the 7th Article after its adoption, which was that "the ratification of the conventions of nine states shall be sufficient for the establishment of this constitution between the states so ratifying the same." It was thus rendered necessarily uncertain whether or not all, or which and what number, would ratify, and if only nine, which would constitute that number. This, therefore, caused a change merely in the style of the expression, to "We, the people of the United States," thereby obviating the difficulty without changing, or intending to change, the meaning; the true sense still being, "We, the people of the several states united." Surely the constitution did not lose its character as a compact by this alteration of the "Committee on Style." Mr. Morris, a member of that committee and the author of the change, afterwards said: "The constitution was a compact, not between individuals, but between political societies; the people not of America, but of the United States, each enjoying sovereign power." Besides, the only way in which the people ordained and established the constitution, was by its "establishment" "*between* the *states*" in ratifying it through their conventions, as provided for in the 7th Article. The people, therefore, named in the preamble, are identified to be the same who, by separate state conventions, established in their ratifications the constitution *between* them. Thus the constitution itself conclusively proves it was not established by the American people "*in the aggregate*," but by separate conventions of the people in their sovereign capacities as states. Not only so, but by the terms, "the establishment of this constitution *between the states*," it defines itself to be a *compact*. Hamilton said in Number 9 of the "Federalist:" "If the new constitution should be adopted, the Union would still be, in fact and in theory, an association of *states*, or a *confederacy*," (the word, *confederacy*, put by himself in capitals). "Will it be said," demanded the "Federalist," "that the fundamental principles have been varied? I ask, What are these principles? Do they require that in the establishment of the constitution the states should be regarded as distinct and independent sovereigns? They are so regarded by the constitution proposed." In number 39 of the "Federalist," it is said: "Each state, in ratifying the constitution, is considered as a sovereign body, independent of all others. The act, therefore, establishing the constitution, will not be a national, but a *federal act*—the act of the people as forming so many independent states; not as forming one *aggregate* nation." Hamilton, in the 85th number of the same work, in speaking of the provisions of the constitution, calls them "The *compacts* which are to *embrace thirteen states*, who are the parties to the *compact*."

The position, that because the federal instrument declares itself to be a constitution, therefore it is not a compact, cannot be maintained. These terms were interchangeable, and were not considered inconsistent with each other at the time of the formation of the government. In the circular (written by Hamilton) of the Annapolis Convention, of 1786, in the address of Congress, responsive to it, and in each and all of the responses of the states to this call for the convention of 1787, the articles of confederation are called the federal *constitution*. In these official documents that instrument is mentioned in all twenty-seven times; and in twenty, out of that number, is called a "*constitution*," as synonymous with "articles of confederation," or "compact."

Mr. Madison, in his letter of 1830 to Mr. Everett, says: "It (the constitution) was formed, not by the governments of the component states, as the federal government, for which it was substituted, * * * nor was it formed by a *majority of the people of the United States*, as *a single community*, in the manner of a consolidated government. It was formed by the states, that is by the people in each state, in their highest sovereign capacity." "The *constitution* is a *compact*." In his letter to Prof. Davis, of 1833, he says: "The federal compact was not formed by individuals as the parties—that is by the people acting *as a single community*—it was formed by the people as separate communities in their sovereign and highest capacity." In his letter, of 1833, to Mr. Webster, in which, while exulting with his distinguished correspondent in his triumph over the nullification and secession doctrine of South Carolina, he expounds to him, with great ability, the true Virginian construction of the constitution of 1798, and closed with these significant words of instruction: "While the constitutional *compact* remains undissolved, it must be executed according to the forms and provisions specified in the *compact*. It must not be forgotten that *compact*, express or implied, is the vital principle of free governments, as contradistinguished from governments not free; and that a revolt against this principle leaves no choice but between anarchy and despotism."

Thus, one cardinal doctrine of the Virginia Proceedings of 1798, viz: that the constitution is a compact between the states, has not only been proven to be true, but great care, it is evident, was taken by the fathers of it, that it should be explained and proclaimed as such; because they considered that feature of it should ever be remembered as one of vital importance.

Another cardinal doctrine recognized and mentioned by those proceedings is, that the constitution creates a division of the powers of sovereignty in a mode which never existed before, in which there is granted to the Federal Government certain specified sovereign powers, to be exercised and enforced through its legislative, judicial, and executive departments; while all other powers of sovereignty not granted, or prohibited, are reserved to the states or the people. The states, while agreeing to this division for the good of all, were so distrustful of the general government, that a majority of them in their ratification proposed amendments to restrict it, or guard it against the exercise of unauthorized powers. Massachusetts proposed 9; South Carolina, 5; New Hampshire, 12; New York, 38; North Carolina, 26; Rhode Island, 21; Virginia, 20. Among those adopted, was article 10, which reads as follows: "The powers not delegated to the United States by the Constitution, nor prohibited by it to the states, are reserved to the states respectively or to the people." This amendment was added by way of precaution against misconstruction, and to proclaim in unmistakable terms such a division of sovereignty to exist. From it, this great truth must result, that on the one side of this division, within the limits of the powers specifically granted in the constitution, the general government alone is sovereign and supreme, and no where else; and on the other hand, outside of those powers therein granted, or prohibited to the states, the latter are equally sovereign and supreme; in other words, while it is true, that, " this constitution and the laws of the United States which shall be made in pursuance thereof, * * shall be the supreme law of the land," it must follow that the laws of the United States, *made not in pursuance thereof*, cannot be the supreme law of the land. It is equally true, that all the laws made by each state within the powers reserved to it by the constitution, must also be the supreme law of the land in that state; for if this is not so, it follows that the 10th Article of the Constitution itself is not supreme. Each state, therefore, is as sovereign in the exercise of its rights within the powers reserved by it, as the general government is sovereign within the powers granted to it.

CHIEF JUSTICE MARSHALL, in delivering the unanimous opinion of the Supreme Court, in the case of *McCulloch* vs. *Maryland*, 4,

Wheaton, said: "In America the powers of sovereignty are divided between the government of the Union and those of the states. They are each sovereign with respect to the objects committed to it; but neither sovereign with respect to the objects committed to the other."

Mr. Madison, in 1835, writes as follows: "It has hitherto been understood that the supreme power, that is, the sovereignty of the people of the states, was in its nature divisible, and was, in fact, divided, according to the Constitution of the United States, between the states in their united, and the states in their individual capacities; that as the states in their highest sovereign character, were competent to surrender the whole sovereignty, and form themselves into a consolidated state, so they might surrender a part and retain, as they have done, the other part forming a mixed "government."

These sovereign powers, as allotted in this division, are thus in general terms described by the "Federalist," in No. 14: "The powers delegated to the Federal Government, are few and defined, and will be exercised principally on external objects as war, peace, negotiation and foreign commerce. The powers reserved to the several states will extend to all those, which, in the ordinary course of affairs, concern the lives, liberties and properties of the people, and the internal order, improvement and prosperity of the state." Virginia, therefore, as has been seen in her proceedings, declared the constitution to be a compact between sovereign states, in which the powers of sovereignty are, in the way we have shown, divided.

She further declared that when the Federal Government, as in the alien and sedition laws, violates that compact, there are only three remedies within its provisions open to the states for relief.

First, the states, as forming the constituent body of the general government, have the right to act as such by co-operation and concert in effecting a repeal of such laws; that to this end, the legislature of each state has the right to interpose a declaration of its opinion on the question of their constitutionality, and by such concurrent action at the recurring elections, the states could elect members in both houses of congress, and a president to conform to their views, and thus gain the desired result through a change in the administration of the government.

Secondly, the question of the validity of such laws might be submitted according to the forms of the constitution to the Federal Judiciary, and if decided unconstitutional, thereby rendered inoperative.

Thirdly, to avoid such laws, amendments to the constitution might be obtained by the action of the states under its 5th article, and the question at issue thus finally settled.

No other remedy than these three were recognized by the Virginia proceedings, except it be the right of revolution, admitted by all, and which could only be justified by such a flagrant violation of the constitution as would produce insufferable wrong.

Such a compact is the constitution; such the sovereignty of the Federal Government; such the sovereignty of the states; and such the doctrine of state rights, as proclaimed by Jefferson and Madison in the Virginia resolutions and report. In them is to be found no ground, or apology whatever, for what is called the right of nullification or secession.

In 1835-6, Mr. Madison wrote as follows: "Although the legislature of Virginia declared, at a late session, almost unanimously, that South Carolina was not supported in her doctrine of nullification by the resolutions of 1798; it appears that those resolutions are still appealed to as expressly or constructively favoring the doctrine." After quoting those resolutions, he asks: "Is there anything from which a single state can infer a right to arrest or annul an act of the general government which it may deem unconstitutional? So far from it, the obvious and proper inference precludes such a right on the part of a single state; the plural number being used in every application of the term." Against the right to secede, he writes in a letter to Mr. Trist, of Dec. 1832: "If one state can at will, withdraw from the others, the others can at will withdraw from her, and turn her *nolentem volentem* out of the Union. * * The essential difference between a free government and governments not free, is that the former is founded in compact, the parties to which are mutually and equally bound by it; neither of them, therefore, can have a greater right to break off from the bargain than the other, or others have to hold them to it. And certainly there is nothing in the Virginia resolutions of 1798, adverse to this principle, which is that of common sense and common justice. The fallacy which draws a different conclusion, lies in confounding a *single* party with the *parties* to the constitutional compact of the United States. The latter having made the compact may do what they will with it. The former, as only one of the parties, owes fidelity to it till released by consent, or absolved by an intolerable abuse of the power created. In the Virginia resolutions and report, the plural number, *states*, is in every instance used where reference is made to the authority which presided over the government. As I am now known to have drawn those documents, I may say, as I do, with a distinct recollection, that the distinction was intentional. It was, in fact, required by the course of reasoning, employed on the occasion. The Kentucky resolutions, being less guarded, have been more easily perverted. The pretext for the liberty taken with those of Virginia, is the word *respective*, prefixed to the rights, etc., to be secured within the states. Could the abuse of the expression have been foreseen, or suspected, the form of it would doubtless have been varied. But what can be more consistent with common sense, than that all having the same rights, etc., should unite in contending for the security of them to each."

In the original draft of the 7th Virginia resolution, where the alien and sedition laws are declared "unconstitutional," following that term were the words "null and void," which, although really used generally as synonymous with unconstitutional, were objected to for fear they might be misconstrued into the semblance of a nullifying act, and were therefore *unanimously* stricken out by the House.

Another significant fact, showing that loyalty to the constitution, and not rebellion against it in any form of nullification, was the grand object of Virginia in her resolutions of 1798, is, that about that time a man by the name of Callender was condemned and imprisoned in Virginia, under the alien and sedition laws, without the least opposition on the part of the State. Indeed, it was said by one of her most distinguished statesmen of that day, the occasion was viewed by Virginia as one for illustrating her devotion to public order, and her acquiescence in laws which she deemed unconstitutional, while those laws were not repealed or pronounced void by the judiciary. These statements are confirmed by the letters from Monroe to Madison, of the 15th of May and the 4th of June, 1800.

Although the term "nullification" is only to be found in the Kentucky resolutions of 1799, (and it is believed not to have been used then in its modern obnoxious sense) it is certain Mr. Madison had nothing to do with *them*. Nor was Mr. Jefferson their author. The resolutions of Kentucky, of which he was the author, were those of 1798, which were drawn by him, and are usually referred to with the Virginia proceedings. They do not contain the term "nullification," or any word equivalent to it. Mr. Madison, in a letter to Mr. Townsend, dated September, 1831, says: "You ask whether Mr. Jefferson was really the author of the Kentucky resolutions of 1799. The fact that he was not, is as conclusive as it is obvious, from his letter to Col. Wilson Cary Nicolas, of Sept. 5, 1799, which expressly declines, for reasons stated, preparing anything for the legislature of that year. * * What might or would have been the meaning attached to the term " nullify " by Mr. Jefferson, is to be gathered from his language in the resolutions of 1798, and elsewhere, as in his letter to Mr. Giles, Dec. 25, 1825. viz: to extreme cases, as alone justifying a resort to any forcible relief. That he ever asserted a right in a single state to arrest the execution of an act of Congress, the arrest to be valid and permanent unless reversed by three-fourths of the states, [the South Carolina doctrine] is countenanced by nothing known to have been said or done by him. In his letter to Major Cartwright, he refers to a convention as a peaceable remedy for conflicting claims of power in our compound government; but whether he alluded to a convention as prescribed by the constitution, or brought about by any other mode, his respect for the will of majorities, as the vital principle of Republican Government, makes it certain that he could not have meant a convention in which a minority of seven states was to prevail over seventeen, either in amending or expounding the constitution."

In their views of all the fundamental principles which are embodied in the American Constitution, and the government over which it was established, none of the great statesmen of the past understood each other better, or were in more perfect accord, than Jefferson and Madison. No more signal proof can be given of this harmony between them, and of their sensitiveness to any alleged difference on these great subjects, than is shown by the letter of the latter in 1833, to "Mutius," in which he says: "Mutius, in his anxiety to discredit the opinions of James Madison, endeavors to discredit the 'Federalist,' in which he bore a part, by observing 'that the work was no favorite with Mr. Jefferson.' Mutius is probably ignorant of, and will be best answered by, the fact that Mr. Jefferson proposed, that with the Declaration of Independence, the Valedictory of General Washington, and the Resolutions and Report of 1798-99, the 'Federalist' should be, as it now is, a text book in the University. He describes it as 'being an authority to which appeal is habitually made by all, and rarely declined or denied by any, as evidence of the general opinion of those who framed, and those *who accepted the Constitution* of the United States, on questions as to its general meaning.' He speaks of the 'Federalist,' 'as being, in his opinion, the best commentary on the principles of government that ever was written.'"

Surely no one can question the authority of Mr. Madison, in his judgment of Mr. Jefferson, and of his opinions, on the political issues of a period in which they were so intimately associated and identified with each other.

Therefore we consider it conclusively settled by the foregoing discussion and authorities, that the right, claimed under the constitution, for a state to nullify an act of the Union, or to secede from it, is wholly adverse to and condemned by the doctrine of state rights, as proclaimed in the Virginia Resolutions and Report of 1798-99.

But we wish in this discussion further to show that by this doctrine of state rights the rightful authority of the Federal Judiciary is fully maintained. Unless this is recognized and enforced our government is a failure.

To understand its jurisdiction correctly, we must be careful in the first instance to discriminate between questions arising under the constitution which are political, and those which are judicial. The decisions of the latter belong exclusively to the judiciary, and when rendered, until reversed by itself, or changed by constitutional amendment, are the supreme law of the land—as supreme as the constitution itself. The decisions of the former belong exclusively to other functionaries of the government, who, respectively, have the right to decide them independently of any dicta of the courts. "The judicial power shall extend to all cases in law and equity arising under the constitution." To be within the authority of the Federal Judiciary under this clause, the case must be one *in law or equity* arising under the constitution. The provision does not say, to all cases arising under the constitution, the laws of the United States and treaties made—but "to all cases *in law and equity* arising," etc.

Congress, in 1798, declared a treaty between the United States and France annulled, on account of violations charged against the latter. Previous to this act, notwithstanding these violations of the treaty by France, the Federal Court, in any case coming before it under that treaty, was bound to recognize it as obligatory, and to enforce the rights of the parties under its provisions. Whether, or not, those violations annulled the treaty, was a political, not a judicial question. It was not one of law or equity, although undoubtedly one arising under the constitution and treaties of the United States. Chief Justice MARSHALL said: "By extending the judicial power to all cases in law and equity, the constitution had never been understood to confer on that department any political power whatever. To come within this description, a question must assume a legal form for forensic litigation and judicial decision. There must be parties to come into the court who can be reached by its process and bound by its powers; whose rights admit of ultimate decision by a tribunal to which they are bound to submit. A case in law or equity may arise under a treaty, when rights of individuals acquired by a treaty, are to be asserted or defended in court. But the judicial power cannot extend to political compacts."

Let us consider briefly, but more especially, the nature of the questions alluded to which are not for the judiciary, but exclusively for other departments of the government to decide.

The constitution provides that "Congress shall have power to make all laws which shall be necessary and proper for carrying into execution the foregoing powers, and all other powers vested by this constitution in the government of the United States, or in any department or office thereof."

Without this provision, the power it expresses would have existed in Congress by implication, but, fearing the system of implied powers, if left without qualification to be inferred, might be used to a dangerous and unwarranted extent, it was thought wise to qualify them by the strong and exclusive words, "necessary and proper." Although these words were used undoubtedly to secure a *strict construction* of the constitution, their application was intended to be practical and to require that, in executing the specified and express powers, Congress should use such means only as are proper and appropriate, and not to be extended to such, which, while they might accomplish the end indirectly, would unduly, and for other purposes, enlarge the power and patronage of the government. All questions arising as to which of the various means, proper and appropriate, should be used for executing the powers referred to in the above clause, are political questions, or matters of policy for Congress alone to decide; because they result from a discretionary power granted to it, with which the judicial department cannot interfere. Questions also exclusively of a political character result from the exercise of discretionary powers granted to the executive department.

In the settlement of these the President has the right to act independently and uncontrolled by either of the other two departments.

It is in reference to the decision of such questions that Mr. Jefferson is to be understood when, in 1819, he writes to Judge Roan as follows: "Each department is truly independent of the others, and has an equal right to decide for itself what is the meaning of the constitution *in the cases* submitted to *its action*, and especially when it is to act *ultimately* and *without appeal*. I will explain myself by examples: A legislature passed the sedition law; the federal courts had subjected certain individuals to its penalties. I released these individuals by the power of pardon committed to executive *discretion*. In the case of *Marbury* vs. *Madison*, the federal judges declared that commissions, signed and sealed by the President, were valid, although not delivered. I deemed delivery essential to complete a deed. I withheld delivery of the commissions. When the British treaty of ——— arrived without any provision against the impressment of our seamen, I determined not to ratify it. The constitution had made their (the Senate's) advice necessary to *confirm* a treaty, but not to reject it. In the cases of two persons *antenati*, under exactly similar circumstances, the federal court had determined that one of them—Duane—was not a citizen; the House of Representatives nevertheless determined that the other—Smith—was a citizen, and admitted him to his seat in their body. Duane was a Republican, and Smith a Federalist, and their decisions were made during the Federal ascendancy. These are examples of my position."

The power of pardon, granted by the constitution, is in its exercise by the executive in all cases a matter of unlimited discretion. In what case and on what ground it is to be exercised, is a political question, and can never be the subject of judicial authority. In the case of *Marbury* vs. *Madison*, on application to the Supreme Court by the former against the latter, for a mandamus to deliver the commissions above referred to, that court *discharged* the rule, which had been served on Mr. Madison, to show cause why that writ should not be issued against him, and decided it had *no right to grant the mandamus, nor any jurisdiction whatever over the case.*

In the case of the treaty, it was surely within the rightful discretion of Mr. Jefferson, as President, to take the initiatory steps either of accepting or rejecting it when submitted to him for his action, and was, therefore, as purely and exclusively a political question for him to decide, as it would have been for the Senate to confirm or reject it, had he submitted it to them for their decision.

In the cases of Duane and Smith, the House of Representatives, in admitting Smith to a seat in their body, notwithstanding the decision of the court against the citizenship of Duane, did no more than exercise the exclusive and discretionary power expressly given them by the constitution to judge of the qualifications of their own members. These examples, cited by Mr. Jefferson expressly to illustrate his true position taken in his letter to Judge Roan and elsewhere, in regard to the right of the executive and the other two departments, each to decide, independently for itself, constitutional questions submitted to them, show conclusively that he only referred to such cases, as by the constitution are brought within the discretion of Congress and the executive, as political questions for the decision of each respectively. They show further, most unquestionably, that he did not intend to refer to cases in law or equity, submitted by the constitution to the decision exclusively of the judiciary. In such cases, the decisions of that department were recognized by both Jefferson and Madison to be final and binding, as rules of action for all the departments of Government, both federal and state.

It is not, however, every measure decided by the Supreme Court as an appropriate means of executing an express power, which is obligatory on either Congress or the Executive to adopt and approve. Undoubtedly, if adopted by Congress and approved by the President, such a measure becomes the supreme law of the land; but if it has expired by its own limitation, or has been repealed, Congress may, in the exercise of its discretion, afterwards adopt it again or not; and should Congress adopt it, the President, in the exercise of a like discretion, may approve or veto it. Because there may be many different constitutional means of executing the same power; in adopting or rejecting any one of which Congress or the Executive would have the right to exercise its discretion. And in so doing, either may be governed by its *own views* of the *constitutionality* of the measure proposed. On this ground, Gen. Jackson could justify himself in vetoing the measure for re-chartering the Bank of the United States, although it had been declared constitutional by the Supreme Court. But a similar discretion does not exist, either in Congress or the Executive, to adopt or reject a measure which, being brought properly before the Supreme Court as a case in law or equity arising under the constitution, has been declared by it to be *unconstitutional.*

After the foregoing necessary explanation of some of the views expressed by Mr. Jefferson, which have been so frequently perverted by ignorance and party prejudice, let us proceed still further to show the real sentiments of the two great authors of the Virginia Proceedings, on the subject of the rightful authority of the federal judiciary. Mr. Madison, in his letter to "Mutius," declares, that "the positions in the report (of 1799) are that the judiciary department is, in all questions submitted to it by the forms of the constitution, to decide in the last resort." In his letter of 1831 to Mr. Trist, he said: "It will not escape notice that the judicial authority of the United States, when overruling that of a state, is complained of as subjecting a sovereign state, with all its rights and duties, to the will of a court composed of not more than seven individuals. This is far from a true state of the case. The question would be between a single state and the authority of a tribunal representing as many states as compose the Union." In 1833 he again wrote: "That the constitution is a compact; that its text is to be expounded *according to the provisions for expounding it* making *a part of the compact;* and none of the parties can rightfully *renounce* the *expounding provision* more than any other part. When such a right accrues, as it may accrue, it must grow out of the abuses of the compact, releasing the sufferers from their fealty to it."

Through the "Federalist," adopted by Jefferson and Madison, as the text book on government, in the University of Virginia, they taught the young men of the country their doctrines on the subject of the Federal Judiciary, so clearly expounded in the following extract from No. 78 of that great work: "The interpretation of the laws is the proper and peculiar province of the courts. A constitution is, in fact, and must be regarded by the judges as a fundamental law.

It must, therefore, belong to them to ascertain its meaning, as well as the meaning of any particular act proceeding from the legislative body. If there should happen to be an irreconcilable variance between the two, that which has the superior obligation and validity, ought of course to be preferred; in other words, the constitution ought to be preferred to the statute, the intention of the people to the intention of their agents. Nor does this conclusion, by any means, suppose a superiority of the judicial to the legislative power. It only supposes that the power of the people is superior to both, and that where the will of the legislature, declared in its statutes, stands in opposition to that of the people, declared in the constitution, the judges ought to be governed by the latter rather than the former. They ought to regulate their decisions by the fundamental laws, rather than by those which are not fundamental." Well may Mr. Jefferson, when he read such words of wisdom, have declared: " In his opinion, the 'Federalist' was the best commentary on the principles of government that ever was written;" and the *Edinburgh Review* responds to such a sentiment by saying: "It exhibits a profundity of research, and accurateness of understanding, which would have done honor to the most illustrious statesmen of ancient or modern times;" and BLACKWOOD'S *Magazine*, also, of 1825, by declaring: " It is a work, altogether, which for comprehensiveness of design, strength, clearness and simplicity, has no parallel. We do not even except those of Montesquieu and Aristotle among the writings of men."

Let us see, now, how far these opinions of the extent of the judicial power of the Federal Government, held by Jefferson and Madison, are maintained by some of the highest authorities known to American jurisprudence.

In *Cohens v. Virginia*, Chief Justice MARSHALL, referring to the 2d Section of the 3d Article of the Constitution, said: " This clause extends the jurisdiction of the court to all the cases described, without making in its terms any exception whatever, and without any regard to the condition of the party. * * A case in law or equity consists of the right of one party as well as of the other, and may truly be said to arise under the constitution, or a law of the United States, whenever its correct decision depends on the construction of either. * *. It (the judicial power) is authorized to decide all cases of every description arising under the constitution, or laws, of the United States. The judicial power of every well constituted government must be *co-extensive with the legislative,* and must be capable of deciding *every judicial question* which grows *out of the constitution and laws.* If any proposition may be considered as a political axiom, this we think, may be so considered."

Judge STORY, in the 2d volume of his Commentaries, declares: "The universal sense of America has decided that, in the last resort, the judiciary must decide upon the constitutionality of the acts and laws of the General and State Governments, so far as they are capable of being made the subject of judicial controversy. It follows that when they are subjected to the cognizance of the judiciary, its judgments must be conclusive; for otherwise they may be disregarded, and the acts of the legislative and the executive enjoy a secure and irresistible triumph. To the people at large, therefore, such an institution is peculiarly valuable, and it ought to be eminently cherished by them. On its firm and independent structure they may repose with safety, while they perceive in it a faculty which is only set in motion when applied to; but, which, when thus brought into action, must proceed with competent power, if required, to correct the error, or subdue the oppression of the other branches of the government. Fortunately, too, for the people, the function of the judiciary in deciding constitutional questions is not one which it is at liberty to decline. It cannot, as the legislative department may, avoid a measure because it approaches the confines of the constitution. It cannot pass it by because it is doubtful. With whatever doubt, with whatever difficulties, a case may be attended, it must decide it when it arises in judgment"

Chancellor KENT says: "Nor is an independent judiciary less useful, as a check upon the legislative power, which is sometimes disposed, from the force of passion, or the temptations of interest, to make a sacrifice of constitutional rights; and it is a wise and neccessary principle of our government, that the legislative acts are subject to the severe scrutiny and impartial interpretation of the courts of justice, who are bound to regard the constitution as the paramount law, and the highest evidence of the will of the people."

"The judicial power of the Union is declared to extend *to all cases* in law or equity arising under the constitution; and *to the judicial power it belongs, whenever a case is judicially before it, to determine what is the law of the land.* The determination of the Supreme

Court of the United States, in *every such case must be final and conclusive*, because the constitution gives to that tribunal the power to decide and gives no appeal from the decision."

Thus, it will be seen, these extracts teach the doctrine of the State Rights' party as taught by Jefferson and Madison, in the Virginia proceedings, in their text book, the "Federalist," and with such emphasis in the correspondence of Mr. Madison, so far as that doctrine relates to the jurisdiction of the Supreme Court. It may be truly said, one great object of that party is not only to enforce the judicial, but all the other powers of the Union, to the fullest extent within the limits which separate them from the reserved powers, and to provide that all along the boundary line of that separation, the several states shall stand as sentinels to guard it by all constitutional means, from being crossed by the forces on either side; for it is the line of liberty and law, of peace and union. The complicity of this government may render the task difficult, but it is no less obligatory. Novel, indeed, our government is in its nature, unlike all others — "the first born" of its kind among the nations of the earth—its powers all beginning and ending in the constitution. Its judicial power comes to it, not as to other goverments by *inheritance or succession*, but created and limited to the words of that instrument. All there is of it, neither more nor less, is embodied in the 3d Article; but within that limit, its judgments, until reversed by itself, or by constitutional amendment, are the supreme law of the land.

Wrong and dangerous positions based on false constructions of the Constitution, have been assumed in critical periods of our history in the name of state rights, which have always met with the condemnation and rebuke of the Democracy. As illustrative of these and as instructive lessons of the past, let us bring a few of them in review before us.

In 1798, the Supreme Court of Pennsylvania, in the case of *The Commonwealth* v. *Cobbet*, by a unanimous opinion first proclaimed the great political heresy afterwards adopted by Massachusetts, Ohio, and South Carolina, viz.: that the constitution of the Union was only a league, without a common arbiter, and that the Supreme Court cannot decide a constitutional question between a State and the General Government. In this case Pennsylvania decided: "If a State differ with the United States, there is no common arbiter but the people, who should adjust the affair by making amendments in the constitutional way, or suffer from the defect. In such a case the Constitution of the United States is Federal; it is a *league* or *treaty* made by individual States as one party, and all the States as another party. There is no provision in the Constitution that in such a case the Judges of the Supreme Court of the United States shall control and be conclusive. Neither can Congress by a law confer that power."

The first instance on record of rebellion by a state against the general Government, was that of Massachusetts during the war of 1812, on the alleged ground that she was justified by the doctrine of state rights and state sovereignty. After six years of insult to our national flag and of outrage to our seamen, committed by England, and patiently endured by America, our then noble and patriotic President, Mr. Madison, in June, 1812, sent to Congress his celebrated war message, in which, among many other wrongs enumerated, he referred to one in the following touching words: "British cruisers have been in the continued practice of violating the American flag on the great highway of nations, and of seizing and carrying off persons sailing under it." This practice, he said, "so far from affecting British subjects alone under the pretext of searching for them, thousands of American citizens under the safeguard of public law and of their national flag, have been borne from their country and from everything dear to them, have been dragged on board ships of a foreign nation, and exposed under the severities of their discipline, to be exiled to the most distant and deadly climes, to risk their lives in the battles of the oppressors, and to be melancholy instruments of taking away those of their own brethren." Congress responded at once to this noble appeal of the President by a declaration of war. Patriot states and patriot men, throughout the land rallied with heart and soul in the cause beneath the national flag, and stood shoulder to shoulder around it. But Massachusetts, faithless among the faithful, interposed her own sovereignty, in deeds and declarations of hostility, to resist the authority and defeat the action of the Federal Government. When the war waged the fiercest and the battles were bloodiest, she publicly denounced her own Government, and apologized for the foe, pleading in defense of her treason, State Rights and State Sovereignty! In June, 1813, both Houses of the Legislature of Massachusetts passed a remonstrance against the war, in which they declare: "The promptness with which Great Britain hastened to repeal her orders before the declaration of war by the United States was known to her, and the restoration of an immense amount of property then within her power, can leave but little doubt that the war on our part was premature, and still less that the perseverance in it after that repeal was known, was *improper, impolitic and unjust.*" Memorials from certain towns in Massachusetts, the three largest of which in population being Newburyport, New Bedford, and Newbury, were referred to a joint committee of the Massachusetts Legislature, whose report was adopted in February, 1814, and in which the committee say, that "the tone and spirit in all of these memorialists are the same," and that the sentiments and feelings expressed in them "are the genuine voice of a vast majority of the citizens of this commonwealth." The memorialists from Newbury, in calling upon the Legislature of Massachusetts for protection against the measures of the Federal Government, make this appeal: "We call upon our state Legislature to protect us in the enjoyment of those privileges to assert which our fathers died, and to defend which we profess ourselves ready to *resist unto blood.* We pray your honorable body to adopt measures immediately to secure to us especially our undoubted right of trade within our state. We are ourselves ready to aid you in securing it to us 'peaceably if we can, forcibly if we must;' and we pledge to you the sacrifice of our lives and property, in support of whatever measures the dignity and liberties of this *free, sovereign and independent state* may seem, to your wisdom, to demand." The committee, in their report, adopted by the Legislature, identifying themselves and a majority in the state with these sentiments, further say, that "They [the committee] believe in the existence of these grievances and in the causes to which they have been ascribed. They believe that this war, so fertile in calamities and so threatening in its consequences, has been waged with the worst possible views, and carried on in the worst possible manner, forming a union of *wickedness and weakness* which defies for a parallel the annals of the world."

In a message of Gov. Strong to the Legislature of Massachusetts, of the 14th of August, 1812, he said: "On the 22d of June I received a letter from Gen. Dearborn, informing me that war was declared against Great Britain, and requesting me to order forty-one companies of the detached militia into the service of the United

States, for the defense of the posts and harbors in this state." * *
"I have been fully disposed to comply with the requirements of the Constitution of the United States and the laws made in pursuance of it, and sincerely regretted that any request could be made by an officer of the National Government to which I *could not constitutionally conform.* But it appears to me that the requisition affixed was of that character, and I was under the same obligation to maintain the *rights of the state* as to support the Constitution of the United States. If the demand was not warranted, I should have violated my duty in a most important point, if I had attempted to enforce it and thereby assisted in withdrawing the militia from the *rightful authority of the state.*" * * "I thought it expedient to convene the Council and request their advice on the subject." * * "The Council advised that they were unable, from a view of the Constitution of the United States and the documents affixed, to perceive that any exigency existed which should render it *allowable to comply with the third requisition.*"

In the report of the joint committee, made February, 1814, above alluded to, which was adopted and approved by the Legislature of Massachusetts, they declare: "The sovereignty reserved to the states was reserved to protect the citizens from *acts of violence by the United States,* as well as for purposes of domestic regulation. We spurn the idea that the *free, sovereign state* of Massachusetts is reduced to a mere municipal corporation, without power to protect its people, and to defend them from oppression from *whatever quarter it comes.* Whenever the national *compact is violated,* and the citizens of this state are oppressed by cruel and unauthorized law, *this Legislature* is bound to *interpose* and wrest from the oppressor his victims. This is the spirit of our Union, and thus has it been explained by the very man [President Madison, who now sets at defiance all the principles of his early political life. The question, then, is not a question of power or right with this Legislature, but of *time and expediency.*" "We know of no surer and better way to prevent that hostility to the Union, the result of oppression, which will eventually terminate in its downfall, than for the wise and good, of those states which have been themselves oppressed, to assemble with delegated authority, and to propose, and even *insist* upon, such explicit declarations of power or instruction as will prevent the most hardy from any future attempts to oppress under the color of the Constitution. This was the mode proposed by Mr. Madison, in answer to objections made as to the tendency of the General Government to usurp upon that of the states; and though he, at a former period, led the Legislature of Virginia into an opposition without any justifiable cause, yet it may be supposed that he, and all others who understood the principles of our concurrent *sovereignty*, will acknowledge the fitness and propriety of their asserting rights which no people can ever relinquish." The report of another joint committee, approved by the Legislature of Massachusetts in October, 1814, declares that she sought a relief "for which the ordinary mode of procuring amendments to the Constitution affords no reasonable expectations in season to prevent the completion of its ruin;" and further, that "the framers of the Constitution made provision to amend defects which were known to be incidental to every human institution, but the *provision itself* was not less liable to be found defective upon experiment than other parts of the instrument;" and that the Government was "*unfit for a state of peace or war.*" Therefore, with no intention of looking to any constitutional mode of relief, the Legislature of Massachusetts, in October, 1814, appointed twelve of her ablest and most distinguished men to attend a convention of representatives of Connecticut and other New England states, to obtain relief from propositions to be made and insisted on by states acting together in their separate and sovereign capacities, in hostility to the Federal Government. A report, signed by the twelve delegates from Massachusetts, viz., George Cabot, Nathan Dane, William Prescott, Harrison G. Otis, Timothy Bigelow, Samuel S. Wilde, George Bliss, Hadigah Baylies, Joseph Lyman, Stephen Longfellow, Joshua Thomas, and Daniel Waldo, was approved by the Legislature of both Massachusetts and Connecticut. In this report Massachusetts, in justification of her course, declared, "It is as much the duty of the *state authorities* to watch over the rights *reserved*, as of the United States to exercise the powers which are delegated." "The Acts of Congress in violation of the Constitution are absolutely void is an undeniable position. It does not consist with the respect and forbearance due from a Confederate State towards the General Government, to fly to open resistance upon *every infraction* of the Constitution. The mode and the energy of the opposition should always conform to the nature of the violation, the intention of the authors, and the extent of the injury inflicted, the determination manifested to persist in it, and the danger of delay. But in cases of deliberate, dangerous and palpable infractions of the Constitution affecting the sovereignty of a state and liberties of the people, it is not only the *right*, but the *duty* of such *a state to interpose* its authority for their protection in the manner best calculated to secure that end. When emergencies occur which are either beyond the reach of the judicial tribunals, or too pressing to admit of delay incident to their forms, *states* which have no common umpire, must be *their own judges, and execute their own decisions.*" This effort of Massachusetts to justify her interposition against the General Government and the war of 1812, was a libel on the Democratic doctrine of State Rights. She appealed neither to the judiciary nor to a Constitutional amendment as a remedy, but abjured both. It was unlawful state resistance to lawful Federal authority. It was not reserved state rights exercised against undelegated Federal power, but state wrongs against Federal rights; not state power in defence of its own sovereignty, but in rebellion against a sovereignty, delegated by itself to another. Such was the the position of Massachusetts in her four years of rebellion against the government during the war of 1812. To know how severely she was condemned by the Democracy of that day, it is only needful to refer to the reports of the joint committees, respectively of the great states of New York and Pennsylvania, made in 1815, on the convention, and its reports above alluded to. The joint committee of the New York Legislature says: "At the time this convention was called, the United States was engaged in a war with one of the most formidable nations on earth. Having terminated hostilities with every other nation, she was bending the whole of her mighty power against our devoted country. Flushed with victory, her minions vauntingly boasted that they would drive our chief magistrate from his station, and bring America a miserable suppliant at the foot of the British throne." * * Referring to the report of that convention, signed by the names which have been given, this committee further say: "it was approved by Massachusetts and Connecticut." "It contains, among other things, a recommendation to the states represented in the convention, to adopt such measures as might effectually protect their citizens from the operation of certain laws, which were then under the consideration of Congress; to unite in an earnest application to the government of the United States to make a surrender to them of a portion of the National revenue, to organize the military force of those states and hold in readiness to act in in their own defense, or that of each other; manifestly for the purpose of resisting the power of the General Government, and finally, if they should be successful in their application, and peace should not be concluded and their defense neglected, as they allege it had been, to appoint delegates to another convention with such power and instructions ' as, (to use their own language) a crisis so momentous might require;' meaning thereby, in the opinion of your committee to *make peace with the enemy, and forcibly to separate themselves from the Union.*"

Another ground of rebellion by Massachusetts against the Federal Government, was the admission of Louisiana into the Union, which she alleged to be a violation of State Rights.

The growth of our country beyond the limits of the old thirteen states to its present grand proportions, owes its origin and progress to the National Democracy. No grander or more patriotic achievement was ever accomplished by them for this high purpose, than the acquisition of Louisiana through their great leader, Thomas Jefferson. Out of this, have come into the Union the important States of Louisiana, Arkansas, Missouri, Kansas and Nebraska, and we may say, Oregon. Previously, this vast territory had been owned, for fifteen years of our national existence, by a powerful foreign nation, which thereby held command of the mouth of the great rivers which rise in our Western States, and flow through them to the Ocean. These outlets to the sea, she had disputed our rights to use, and thus our commerce was endangered and our trade restricted. On this splendid achievement of Mr. Jefferson—this grant of the freedom of the seas to our commerce—this peaceful purchase, not by blood, but for a paltry sum, of this vast domain and of these highways to the Ocean—this one great occasion of our national expansion and of our national glory—Massachusetts charged the government with having committed a great wrong, and made the admission of Louisiana into the Union one of the counts in her indictment against the Federal Government during the war of 1812. She charged that admission to be a violation of state rights, and flagrantly so, as it had been done without obtaining the assent of *each* and *all the states* as *members* of the national *compact*. She therefore instructed her

Senators and Representatives in Congress, more than a year after its passage, to repeal this act of admission and thus to dissolve the union formed with the new state, because she charged it was in violation of state rights and state sovereignty. Although the acquisition of Louisiana, and its admission as a State in the Union, had been declared constitutional by the Supreme Court, and by all the departments of the government, and sustained by the nation at large, as an act of the highest statemanship; yet on the occasion of the annexation of Texas, in 1844, Massachusetts, actuated by the same rebellious spirit against the Federal Government, which characterized her opposition to the admission of Louisiana into the Union, assumed a rebellious position, and threatened the exercise of state sovereignty against the Federal Government by declaring, " that the project of the annexation of Texas, unless arrested on the threshold, may drive these states into a dissolution of the Union." "And as the powers of legislation, granted in the Constitution of the United States to Congress, do not embrace the case of the admission of a foreign state by the legislature—such an act of admission would have no binding force whatever on the people of Massachusetts."

Ohio, by a resolution of her Legislature, passed in the winter of 1820-21, declared: " This General Assembly do recognize and approve the doctrine asserted by the Legislatures of Kentucky and Virginia, in their resolutions of November and December, 1798, and January, 1800, and do consider that their principles have been recognized and adopted by a majority of the American people. " At the same time, in violation of those Virginia principles, she adopted the report of the Committee who presented the resolution, in which, referring to the Bank of the United States, they " recommend that provision be made by law forbidding our Courts, Justices of the Peace, Judges and Grand Juries from taking any cognizance of any wrong alleged to have been committed upon any species of property owned by the Bank, or upon any of its corporate rights or privileges; and prohibiting our Notaries Public from protesting any notes or bills by the Bank or their agents or made payable to them." This Bank was a constitutional fiscal agent of the General Government, decided to be such by the Supreme Court. The law commended in the report rendered the Bank wholly inoperative and therefore an act of nullification, placing Ohio in direct hostility to the Federal Government, and, classing her with Pennsylvania and Massachusetts as the only States in the union which up to 1821 had taught the doctrine that the Constitution was only a league, and had nullified an act of Congress and ignored the authority of the Federal Judiciary.

Equally condemned by the Democracy, is the extreme doctrine of state rights advocated by the Hon. William Rawle, a most distinguished jurist of Pennsylvania, the author of one of the earliest and most celebrated commentaries on the Constitution. He was born in Philadelphia in 1759. Having studied law in New York, in London, and in Paris; having been offered by Washington the Attorney-Generalship of the United States, and served as District Attorney and as Chancellor of the Bar Association of Philadelphia; he published, in 1825, a commentary on the constitution which has been circulated, ever since its publication, far and wide througout the Union. This work is quoted by Judge Story as one of the earliest and highest authorities on many questions of constitutional law. Considering its early date and its high standing and extensive circulation, perhaps no commentary has exerted a greater influence in construing the Constitution than that of the renowned jurist of the Philadelphia Bar. In his celebrated commentary, he virtually justifies the heresy of his own State which has been cited, by assuming the position that "the secession of a State from the Union depends on the will of the people of such state." In other words, that without an actual violation by the General Government of the Federal compact, a state has not only the right to interpose, but even to secede. Such a doctrine as that maintained by Rawle, and by the different states on the occasions which have been named is wholly inconsistent with, and condemned by, the State Rights creed of 1798, and by that advocated by the National Democracy of the present day.

South Carolina in 1833 followed these precedents, and made herself prominent in the support of such heresies, which were promptly disclaimed by Virginia, in her resolutions of that year denouncing them, and were bravely resisted by the National Democracy headed by General Jackson, then their distinguished leader and President.

The next example which we shall notice in this connection is the case of *Rhode Island* v. *Massachusetts*, in which Rhode Island filed a bill in the Federal Court against Massachusetts, asking for the establishment of the Northern boundary between the two States, and the right of the complainant to a tract of land in dispute, containing about eighty square miles. Notwithstanding the plain, express provision of our Constitution that the judicial power shall extend "to controversies between two or more States," and that the General Government, even under the old Articles of Confederation, had the express authority to settle such disputes "as may arise between two or more States concerning *boundary*," Massachusetts moved to dismiss the bill on the ground that the Court had no jurisdiction of the cause, because of her *State Rights and State Sovereignty*. She dared boldly to declare before that high National tribunal in all the pride of her Stately power, that " this suit being for *sovereignty* and *sovereign rights*, is *beyond* the jurisdiction of a *judicial court*." "The common law of England takes no jurisdiction over the actions of Sovereign States, nor is there any power in Chancery to hold jurisdiction over a Sovereign, without his consent. Such is the character of the States, respectively, of this Union " "The States never intended to include in their controversies questions of *sovereign right*, for the regulation of which no law is made, and no law ever can be made by any other power than themselves, *and each one for itself*." Fortunately, the little but plucky State of Rhode Island was the party present to rebuke such sovereign audacity. When Massachusetts expressed the hope that if the Court should decide against her, "it will, for the honor of the Court, for the honor of the country, be sure to find some way to *execute its decree*;" Rhode Island promptly responded: "What! does Massachusetts threaten? Is Massachusetts ready to become a nullifying State, and to set up her will in defiance of this Court and of the Constitution?" After such stormy words from Rhode Island, with perchance a slight suggestion that General Jackson was still alive, the record becomes suddenly silent as to the final result of the controversy.

In the course of events, the great American conflict of 1860, occurred. Its issues and results necessarily demand our attention in the discussion of the subject under consideration.

The Southerners claimed the exercise of two rights, which they alleged were of vital interest to them, and were secured by the Federal Constitution.

The *first* was, the equal right of the people of the United

States, without discrimination, to emigrate, with whatever property they possessed, including slaves, to any common territory, not embraced in the ordinance of '87, and to be secure in its peaceable enjoyment until each territory might be admitted as a state into the Union, with or without slavery, as she might determine.

The *second* was, the right to the execution of the clause in the constitution which provides that " no person, held to service or labor in one state under the laws thereof, escaping into another, shall in consequence of any law or regulation therein, be discharged from such service, or labor, but shall be delivered up on claim of the party to whom such service or labor may be due."

The denial of those rights to the South by the Republican party formed the great issues of 1860.

The Democratic party of the North advocated them, not because they were in favor of slavery or wished to perpetuate it, but because these were rights existing in the constitution which by their honor and their oath they were bound to support. In this they had only followed the Fathers who had formed the constitution for the thirteen states, twelve of which were slave states whose citizens from the time of its adoption and through all the administrations of Washington, Adams, Jefferson and Madison, had exercised these rights without hindrance from State or Federal authority but with the aid and concurrence of both.

Let us now look back, to some extent, into the history of American slavery, and of the political events connected with it, in order that we may weigh more justly the responsibilities of the parties of to-day for the great conflict, which resulted from the issues we have named, and see more clearly the present positions of each.

Let it be understood, however, in advance, that while we condemn the South for its separation from the North, we arraign the Republican party for its follies and crimes in all they did to provoke it, and commend the Democratic party of the North for all they did to avoid it.

Let us acknowledge, also in advance, that out of the evil deeds of the Republican party, and the great error of the South, Providence, as it often does, has made the wrath and wickedness of man to praise Him. To Him, and Him alone, working through the wicked ambition and folly of man, and not through the benevolence of the Republican party, is the black man indebted to his freedom, and the South for its relief from the burden of slavery.

For the origin and existence in the past of American slavery, Massachusetts is to-day more responsible than South Carolina. England is more responsible than them both, or, than the North and South combined. She not only taught it as consistent with the precepts of our religion, but forced it upon her colonies against their earnest protestations. Through her leading commentators and theologians, she taught that slavery, like sickness and poverty, was incident to the fall of man, and therefore ineradicable; that it is not sin in itself, but only in its abuse, like any other relation of life: that God, in His theocracy, in the decalogue itself, not only recognized slavery amongst the Jews, but, by Divine decree, authorized them to buy slaves from the heathen, and perpetuate their servitude from generation to generation—declaring the slave to be his owner's "money"; that in the times of the Apostles, their Lord lived in the midst of slaveholders, to whose authority he commanded obedience; that while he gave sight to the blind, hearing to the deaf, health to the sick, and life to the dead, and dared denounce the Scribes and Pharisees for their hypocrisy and adultery, he gave no freedom to the slave, nor did he denounce the slaveholder as a wrong-doer: but on application healed for the Centurion his dying slave, and restored him to service without a plea for his freedom, or a rebuke to his master. Indeed, England's latest and most distinguished scholars and commentators, Alford, Conybear and How son, shrink not from teaching that Paul returned a fugitive slave to his master, and that the passage in which the Apostle says: "Art thou called being a servant, care not for it; but if thou mayest be made free, use it rather;" is an admonition to a slave to be content with his lot, and to use it, slavery, rather than change his condition. In 1711, the Commons of England resolved, that "the plantations ought to be supplied with negroes at reasonable rates." In 1713, England, by contract resulting from the treaty of Utretcht,. engaged to supply certain portions of America annually, for thirty years, with 4,800 slaves. Shortly afterward, the Crown in council submitted to the Twelve Judges of England the question: what was the legal *status* of negro slaves in the hands of British subjects? The response was: "In pursuance of his Majesty's order, in council, hereunto annexed, we do humbly certify our opinion to be that negroes are *merchandise*," signed by Lord Chief Justice Holt and nine other Judges! After this, negro slaves were largely owned in

England, and were frequently sold on the public exchange in London. The merchants of London, on one occasion, submitted to Sir Philip Yorke, afterward Lord Hardwicke, and to Lord Talbot, who were the Solicitor and the Attorney General of the Kingdom, this question: "What are the rights of a British owner of slaves in England?" Their answer was: "A slave coming from the West Indies to England, with or without his master, doth not become free, and the master may legally compel him to return to the plantation." In 1749, the same question again came up before Sir Philip Yorke, then Lord Chancellor of England, and by a decree in chancery he affirmed the same doctrine. In 1771, Lord Mansfield, in the Sommersett case, so far dissented from the opinions of Lord Hardwicke and others, as to decide, not that a slave brought from America to England thereby became forever free, but that *such a law* of slavery as was in force in *Jamaica*, or the *West Indies*, could not operate in England, and there was no remedy to compel the slaves' return. With the view of showing what was the character of that African slavery which, as defined by the laws of England, she established by force in her colonies, let us quote from a review of the Sommersett decision, by Lord Stowell, of whom Lord Brougham has said: "Seldom if ever appeared in the profession of the law any one so peculiarly endowed with all the learning and capacity which can accomplish, as well as all the graces which can embellish, the judicial character, as this eminent person." Lord Stowell, in the case of the slave Grace, (decided in 1827), said: "The arguments of counsel, in that decisive case of Sommersett, do not go further than to the extinction of slavery *in England*, as unsuitable to the genius of this country, and to the modes of enforcement. It is observable that Lord Mansfield limits it (the question) expressly to *this country*, for he says: 'The *now* question is, whether any dominion, authority, or coercion, can be exercised on a slave in *this country*, according to the American laws; meaning thereby the laws of the West Indies.' In the final judgment he delivers himself thus: 'The state of slavery is so odious, that nothing can be suffered to support it but positive law.' That is slavery *as it existed* in the *West Indies*, for it is to that he looks, considering that many of the adjuncts that belonged to it *there*, were not admissible under the laws of England." To the above declaration that slavery cannot be established without positive law, which he calls an *obiter dictum*, Lord

Stowell replies: "That ancient custom is generally recognized as a just foundation of all law; that villenage of both kinds, which is said by some to be the prototype of slavery, had no other origin than ancient custom; that a great part of the common law itself, in all its relations, has little other foundation than the same custom; and that the practice of slavery as it exists in Antigua and several other of our colonies, though regulated by law, has been in many instances founded upon a similar authority." Having thus overruled this *obiter dictum*, as he calls it, of Lord Mansfield, he says: "The fact certainly is, that *it never has happened*, that the slavery of an African, returned from England, has been interrupted in the colonies in consequence of this sort of *limited liberation* conferred upon him in England. The entire change of the legal character of individuals, produced by the change of local situation, is far from being a novelty in the law. Persons bound by particular contracts which restrain their liberty, debtors, apprentices, and others, lose their character and condition for the time when they reside in another country, and are entitled as persons totally free; though they return to their original servitude and obligations upon coming back to the country they had quitted. Having adverted to most of the objections that arise to the revival of slavery in the colonies, I have first to observe that it returns upon the slave by the same title by which it grew up originally. It never was in Antigua the creature of *law*, but of that *custom* which operates with the force of law: and when it is cried out that *malus abolendus est*, it is first to be proved that, even in the consideration of England, the use of slavery is considered as a *malus usus*, which the Court of the King's Privy Council and the Courts of Chancery are every day carrying into full effect in all considerations of property, in the one by appeal, and in the other by original causes, and all this enjoined by statutes. Has it not [that is the government], since the declaration of its judgment against slavery, declared in the most explicit and authentic manner its encouragement of slavery in its colonial establishments? Have not innumerable acts passed which regulate the condition of slaves, and which tend to consider them as the colonists themselves do, *res posito in commercio*, as mere goods and chattels, as subject to mortgages, as constituting part of the value of estates, as liable to be taken in execution for debt, to be publicly sold for such purposes, and has it not established courts of the highest jurisdiction for carrying into execution provisions for all these purposes? Can it be asserted that the law of England does not support, and in a high degree favor, the law of slavery in its West India Colonies—however it may discourage it in the Mother Country? If it be a sin, it is a sin in which this country has had its full share of guilt."

Lord Stowell sent a copy of this opinion to Judge Story, of Massachusetts, then a Justice of the Supreme Court of the United States; who in a letter, dated Salem, near Boston, Sept. 22, 1828, replies: " I have read with great attention your judgment in the slave case. Upon the fullest consideration which I have been able to give the subject, I entirely concur in your views. If I had been called upon to pronounce a judgment in a like case, I should certainly have arrived at the same result, though I might not have been able to present the reasons which led to it in such a striking and convincing manner. It appears to me that the decision is impreguable In my native State (Mass.), the state of slavery is not recognized as legal; and yet if a slave should come hither and afterwards return to his home, we should certainly think that the local law would re-attach upon him." Such was the system of slavery in England, as expounded by her divines, her law-makers, and judges, which she had by her tyranny forced upon her colonies, and of which, when they became Independent States, they found themselves the victims.

As early as 1760, South Carolina passed an act forbidding the importation of slaves, which was rejected by the King; and her Governor reprimanded. Virginia, in 1770, passed a similar act with a like result. In 1775, just on the eve of the revolution, the Earl of Dartmouth, in reply to a remonstrance from the agent of the colonies against the importation of slaves, said: " We cannot allow the colonies to check or discourage a traffic so beneficial to the nation."

After the peace of 1783, the first act by the states in their collective capacity, containing a restriction against slavery, was the celebrated ordinance of 1787, passed by the Congress of the Confederation for the " Territory north-west of the Ohio;" the 6th Article of which excluded slavery from that territory, with this provision: " Provided always that any person escaping into the same, from whom labor or service is lawfully claimed in any one of the original states, such fugitive may be lawfully reclaimed and conveyed to the person claiming his or her labor or service as aforesaid." Mr. Poole, a native of Massachusetts, in his able piece in the *North American Review*, for April, 1876, proves conclusively that Mr. Dane, of that state, although reputed to be, was not the author of that ordinance. On the other hand, Mr. Peter Force, the late president of the National Institute at Washington, and author of the ten volumes of "American Archives," in his article in the *Western Law Journal*, of 1848, has shown most satisfactorily that Mr. Carrington, of Virginia, chairman of the committee who reported it, was really its author. It is true, Mr. Dane, after he had joined in its report, *without* the slavery clause, when he found the House in favor of such a restriction, and *not until then*, did move the 6th Article as an amendment. Three days after its adoption he wrote to Mr. Rufus King, saying: "I had no idea the states would agree to the 6th Article, prohibiting slavery, as only Massachusetts of the eastern states was present, and, therefore, omitted it in the draft, but finding *the House* favorably disposed on the subject, after we had completed the other parts, I moved the Article, which was agreed to without opposition." On its passage, there were eight states represented, five southern and three northern. The delegates from the South, wanting but one of being double of those from the North, unanimously voted for it; the only opposition being among the few northern delegates, who cast merely six votes in its favor. In July, 1787, while the passage of this ordinance was under consideration, Dr. Cutler, a man on whom Yale had conferred the degree of LL.D., who had taken regular degrees in law, divinity, and medicine, and was four years in Congress from Dane's district, was sent as the agent of a company organized for holding lands in the north-west, to urge the passage of a suitable act for its government. Although not there when the ordinance was reported and passed, he had previously frequent interviews with all the members of the committee on the subject. In his diary, kept at that time, he writes: "Dane must be carefully watched, notwithstanding his professions." "Grayson, R. H. Lee, and Carrington are certainly my warm advocates. Lee tells me he has a speech an hour long prepared." The great principles of free government, such as the right of trial by jury, the benefits of the writ of *habeas corpus*, of religious liberty, the encouragement of public schools, etc., etc., which are contained in the ordinance, are in wonderful harmony with those to be found scattered through the earlier constitutions of Virginia and North Carolina, adopted in 1776; and go far to confirm the reasoning and newly discovered testimony of Mr. Force, to prove that it was emphatically a measure of Southern origin.

It may be added just here, that Rufus King, in the Congress of 1785, when the Northern states were in the majority, had moved a clause prohibiting slavery in this territory, as an amendment to the ordinance of Mr. Jefferson, which had already passed without it; but that majority merely "committed it," and, although certainly having the power, failed even to call it up, or attempt to pass it.

In part explanation of this apathy in the enactment of the ordinance on the part of New England, Mr. Poole, in the article above referred to, very significantly says: "The Massachusetts members never engaged with much zeal in any plan for settling the north-western territory. They saw it would draw away the capital of their own state, and thousands of its most enterprising citizens, as it did. Massachusetts had an immense unoccupied territory, in the province of Maine, on the market, and Maine was a part of her own jurisdiction." Hence, Dr. Cutler's distrust of Mr. Dane. Hence, neither he, nor any one from his state, ever called up Mr. King's amendment, nor offered any one like it, to ordinances reported for the North-west by committees of which he was a member, and when all New England was present. Hence, he did not propose the 6th Article which was passed, until prompted *by the House*. Besides, he was utterly incapable of writing such an ordinance, as shown conclusively by Mr. Poole. He was then but thirty-four years old, had received his education very late in life, had practiced law but five years, and, as his biographer says, was always ungraceful and awkward in the style of his composition. On the other hand, Carrington, the chairman, who reported the ordinance, was a man of experience and of marked talent and ability; and Lee, his colleague and assistant in the committee, was one of the most distinguished men in America. In 1776, he had been selected to move for adoption the resolution of Independence; and his speech on that memorable occasion to his high auditory, is said to have been one of transcendant power, a marvel of eloquence and oratory, producing a scene of excitement and passion unknown before in so grave an assemblage. After this, he became a member of Congress, over which he was elected to preside.

Is it conceivable that Carrington and Lee, men of such great talents and experience, would have resigned the task of framing such an ordinance, requiring the highest order of statesmanship, for an original part of Virginia, to a young, inexperienced lawyer, like Dane, of only five years' practice, and wholly unknown to the public at that time as an author? Such a statement is incredible. And it is said, Mr. Webster, after his celebrated eulogy upon the ordinance, was convinced of his error in supposing that Dane was its author. Drafted, therefore, by Virginia, for the government of the territory she had ceded, and enacted by a Congress in which the Southerners had an overwhelming majority, almost two to one, in which they gave it their unanimous support, why was it that the ordinance, thus voted for, contained a restriction against slavery, hitherto unheard of in the legislation of the country? The only true answer to this question is to be found in the following explanation: Virginia, both before and after the Revolution, had been the most prominent and zealous of all the states in her persistent efforts to prohibit the importation of slaves from abroad; and it was to shut the door of this vast territory against the introduction of such importations, rather than against the slaves already in America, which induced Virginia and the other states to adopt so unanimously the 6th Article of the ordinance. A contrary motive, with other considerations which have been named, may have induced the commercial states of New England, whose citizens had engaged so extensively in the slave trade, to postpone indefinitely the adoption of Mr. King's proposition, and to be so dilatory and careless about the passage of such a measure. For it is true, as Judge McLean, in one of his judicial opinions, said: "This system of slavery was imposed upon our colonial settlements by the Mother Country, and it is due to truth to say, that the commercial colonies and states were chiefly engaged in the traffic." The contrast between the apathy of those states and the zeal of Virginia, in their opposition to the slave trade, was manifestly shown in deciding the question in the convention of 1787 whether it should be discontinued in 1800, or continued until 1808. Massachusetts, New Hampshire, and Connecticut voted for its continuance to 1808, and *Virginia* that it should not be continued beyond 1800. That the above was the purpose and policy which caused the insertion of the 6th Article in the ordinance of '87, is conclusively proven by Mr.

Madison, who, in his letters of 1819 and 1820, to Mr. Walsh and President Monroe, wrote as follows: "The great object of the convention seemed to be to prohibit the increase of the *importation* of slaves. A power to emancipate slaves was disclaimed. Nor is anything recollected that denoted a view to *control the disposition* of those *within* the country. When the existence of slavery in that (the north-western) territory was precluded, the importation of slaves was *rapidly going on*, and the only mode of checking it was by narrowing the space open to them. The expedient would not have been undertaken, if the power afterwards given to terminate the importation everywhere had existed, or been even anticipated. When the ordinance passed, the Congress had no authority to prohibit the importation from abroad. All the states had, and some were in the full exercise of, the right to import them, and consequently there was no mode, in which Congress could check the evil, but the indirect one of narrowing the space open for the reception of slaves. Had a federal authority then existed to prohibit directly and totally the importation from abroad, can it be doubted that it would have been exerted? and that a regulation having merely the effect of prohibiting an interior disposition of the slaves actually in the United States, would not have been adopted, or perhaps thought of?" Mr. Madison was simultaneously a member of the old Congress and of the convention of 1787. The fourth volume of the Journal of the Continental Congress shows him to have been present in that body on the 14th of July, 1787, the day after the passage of the ordinance, and to have made a report in conjunction with Carrington, Dane, and King, on the subject of the north-western territory: and his works show that during all these proceedings in relation to it, by letters, dated at that time, he was in correspondence with Jefferson and others on the subject. It was Mr. Madison who, in the convention of '87, on the 18th of August, first moved for a constitutional provision "to dispose of the unappropriated lands of the United States, and to institute temporary governments for new states arising therein;" which suggestion led to the adoption of the provisions now in the constitution relating to the power of Congress over the territories, and the admission of new states. He was also a member of the first Congress, which, in 1789, passed the act to continue in full effect the ordinance of '87. Who, then, can challenge his high authority on all questions which relate to this ordinance, and the constitutional provisions and legislative action which followed it on the subject of the territories? In his letter to Mr. Walsh he says: "It may be observed that the ordinance, giving its distinctive character on the subject of slaveholding, proceeded from the old Congress acting with the best intentions, but *under a charter* which contains no shadow of the authority exercised."

Seemingly conscious of this truth, its authors founded it, in fact and form, in the nature of a compact which should be considered binding on all the states consenting to it, either expressly or by acquiescence, as they certainly did. For the same original sovereignty of the separate states, which united, formed the confederacy, could, with equal authority, adopt the ordinance as a binding compact.

Adopted thus, before the existence of our present constitution, its obligatory force was recognized and continued by the following clause in that instrument: "All debts contracted, and *engagements* entered into, *before* the adoption of this constitution, shall be as valid against the United States under the constitution as under the confederation." By virtue of this clause, the ordinance, as an engagement valid against the United States, was perpetuated, but to the extent only of its existence over the territories embraced by it, *so long* as they remained such; for by one of its own provisions, each state formed out of them "shall be admitted by its delegates into the Congress of the United States *on an equal footing* with *the original states.*" By this provision, the ordinance itself provided for its own annulment when the territories it governed were admitted as states into the Union under the present constitution. For in the act of admission, they were invested with the same powers which the original states had. Congress, thus bound by an engagement existing prior to the constitution, passed, in compliance with it, acts applying the ordinance with its restriction against slavery to the several territories into which the North-west included in it was divided, viz., to the territory of Indiana in 1800, to that of Ohio in 1802, to that of Michigan in 1805, to that of Illinois in 1809, and to that of Wisconsin in 1836.

In accordance with the construction of the constitution, that no authority existed in it, outside the ordinance, for congress to apply the restriction against slavery to any territory of the United States, the General Government, in all its departments, had refrained from the exercise of such a power, and Congress had always disclaimed it, up to the enactment of the Missouri compromise in 1820. The act of the first congress, containing many of the members of the old congress, and of the convention of 1787, passed in 1790 for the government of the territory of Tennessee, applied to it some of the provisions of the ordinance, but expressly excepted the restriction against slavery. So with the act of 1798 for the government of the Mississippi territory; during the passage of which, a Mr. Thatcher moved the restriction, as an amendment, when Mr. Otis of Massachusetts said: "He hoped the motion would not be withdrawn, and the reason why he wished this, was that an opportunity might be given to gentlemen who came from the same part of the Union with him to manifest that it is not their disposition to interfere with the Southern states, as to the species of property in question. By permitting slavery in this district of country, the number of slaves would not be increased, and he could see nothing in the transit of slaves from slave states into the territory, which could affect the philanthropy of his friend." Mr. Gallatin, of Pennsylvania, said: "By the laws of the different states, the importation of slaves is prohibited, but if this amendment does not obtain, he knows not how slaves could be precluded from being introduced (from abroad) by way of New Orleans, not then a part of the United States. He hoped, *therefore*, the amendment would be agreed to." The amendment was overwhelmingly voted down, and received but twelve votes. So in the act of 1804 for the government of Louisiana; in the act of 1805 for the government of the Orleans territory; and in that of 1812 for the government of the Missouri territory. In each and all of these acts, Congress had, up to 1820, disclaimed, by refusing to exercise it, any right under the constitution to extend the restriction against slavery beyond the provision made for it in the ordinance of 1787. Mr. Madison, in confirmation of his own opinion of the unconstitutionality of such a restriction, bears testimony to this uniform practice of Congress against it, through all the administrations of the fathers, through those of Washington, Adams, Jefferson and his own, down to his successors. Judge McLean, in his dissenting opinion of 1856, alludes to this statement, when he says: "In a late re-publication of a letter of Mr. Madison, dated November 27, 1819, speaking of this power of Congress to prohibit slavery in a territory, he infers there is *no such power*, from the fact that it has not been exercised." Congress had, by various acts, in regard to the shipping, and to the territories, endeavored as far as possible, to restrict the foreign slave trade, previous to 1808, consistently with the provision in the Constitution for its discontinuance in all the states. That provision had been uniformly construed to apply by its express words, only in favor of the *states* which "shall think proper to admit" such person, but not to include the *territories*. Congress, therefore, as early as 1798, prohibited their importation into a territory; and afterwards, by the act, for the Louisiana or Orleans territory, prohibited the importation of such slaves directly into that territory, or of those who had been imported elsewhere since 1798, except by American citizens who shall settle in such territory; for in that year Congress had passed the prohibitory act referred to, and, as we have seen, Mr. Gallatin stated, the different states had, at that time, prohibited the importation of slaves. From the power "to regulate commerce among foreign nations," Congress derived the right to prohibit the commerce in slaves, between the *states*, and such nations, after 1808, and, from the same express power, the right to prohibit either the direct or indirect importation of slaves from abroad into the territories, either *before or after* 1808. These acts, therefore, cannot be considered in the least inconsistent with the opinion of Mr. Madison and the uniform practice of congress and the fathers in conformity to it from 1789 to 1820, viz.: that it was unconstitutional for Congress to apply the 6th Article of the ordinance of 1787 to territories not embraced by it.

In the Congress of 1818, a bill was introduced for the admission of Missouri into the Union. The 6th Article of the Ordinance of '87 was moved as an amendment to the bill, and its insertion in her constitution made a condition to her admission. The House passed the bill thus amended. The Senate rejected it. The two houses failing to agree on the question raised by the amendment, no bill for the admission of Missouri was passed at that session. During the next Congress, on the 9th of December, 1819, a similar bill was introduced in the House, and, with a like amendment proposed, passed that body on the 1st of March, 1820. On the 3d of January, 1820, a bill for the admission of Maine passed the House, whilst the Missouri bill with its restrictive amendments was pending in that body, which had become the subject of stormy and violent debate. The Senate having, as at the previous session, a decided majority against such a restriction, which it was determined to reject, adopted two amendments to the bill for the admission of Maine. One proposed by Mr. Thomas, of Illinois, as a compromise, provided for a division of the territory outside of Missouri by the line of 36° 30'—north of which slavery was forbidden, and south of which it was allowed—a compromise having reference to a subject different from the admission of Missouri, namely, the settlement of future difficulties that might arise in disposing of other questions than the one then on hand. It was not offered by a majority of the Senate as a compromise to settle the restriction against Missouri, to which they were irreconcilably opposed; nor received as such by the majority of the House, who were in favor of that restriction; but as the settlement of a distinct subject, on which the sense of Congress had never been taken; as a compromise standing on its own independent basis, having its own supposed equivalents within itself, and in which the consideration given to the North, as stated at the time by Mr. Kinsey, of New Jersey, and its other northern friends, greatly preponderated by securing to it nine-tenths of the divided territory. But the other amendment provided for the cotemporaneous admission of Missouri and Maine; and was a measure resorted to by the Senate, to unite the friends of Maine in the House with the anti-restrictionists of that body, and thus defeat the restrictionists. No compromise on that subject was offered them, but this combination was sought to overcome their majority in the House. Both of these amendments were rejected by the House. The Senate *insisted* on them and the House *insisted* on its *disagreement* Both houses then concurred in appointing committees of conference. On the 2d of March, Mr. Holmes, of Massachusetts, Chairman of the House Conference Committee, made his report, which was that the Senate should *recede* from its two amendments to the Maine bill, thus leaving Maine disconnected; that the two houses should pass the Missouri House bill, first striking out the slavery restriction clause, and substituting therefor the Thomas provision. A like report was made to the Senate, and agreed to without count. The first action of the house on the report was on the proposition to strike from it the Missouri restriction, which was carried by a vote of ninety to eighty-seven, a mere majority of *three*.

This was the *test vote*, on which the ayes and noes were recorded. Next came up the Thomas provision, which was carried by a vote of one hundred and thirty-four to forty-two. This last vote, by the rules, passed the bill through the House and made its action final. Of the ninety who voted against the restriction on Missouri, only *fourteen* were from the North—ten of whom were from Massachusetts, Connecticut, Rhode Island, and New Jersey, including four from Massachusetts; all of these closely connected in their relationship to Maine, and interested in her success. The conclusion from these facts is irresistible, that the separation of Maine, and her admission as an important part of the plan conceded by the anti-restrictionists, and commended by the Committee of Conference, turned the scale and obtained a majority of *three* in favor of Missouri. Her admission was thus secured by no other compromise than that contained in a combination of *her* friends with the friends of Maine for their mutual success. The party of restrictionists who had struggled so uncompromisingly against her, of course joined, after this defeat, in sustaining the Thomas provision, which they had previously rejected, as the only restriction now left for them to vote for, and as the next best thing to do. Hence the large majority it obtained of one hundred and thirty-four to forty-two.

A small majority of the Southerners voted in the affirmative, and nearly all of those in the negative were from the South, who were decided in their convictions that the territorial, as well as the state restriction, was *unconstitutional*. In confirmation of the above views, Mr. Clay, in 1850, said: "In the Senate a majority was opposed to such restriction. In the Senate, therefore, in order to carry Missouri through, a provision for her admission *was coupled with the bill for the admission of Maine*. They were connected, and the Senate said to the House: 'You want the bill for the admission of Maine passed. You shall not have it unless you take along with it the bill for the admission of Missouri also.'" One of the ablest and boldest speeches Mr. Clay ever made was in ,the House on that occasion, when he appealed to the friends of Maine, and assured them that if they did not join in the defeat of the Restrictionists, and allow the young Western State to enter into the Union on an equal footing with the one from the East, Maine would not be admitted.

Not more wonderful was the error, pointed out by Mr. Clay in 1850, which he said had prevailed so long, not only in the Senate, but throughout the country, in reference to the authorship of the compromise line of 36° 30´; than is that other stupendous falsehood uttered by Republicans in all their campaigns of the past and of to-day, in direct contradiction of the records of Congress, which charges that the party, known in 1820 as the Restrictionists, consented to vote for the admission of Missouri into the Union without the restrictive clause, on the pledge given that the South would vote for the Thomas amendment; whereas, Missouri, as we have shown, was admitted against their uncompromising opposition and for no such consideration at all. After the act for the admission of Missouri had passed, and she had fully complied with its provisions, she applied in December, 1820, to Congress for recognition as a state in the Union. This was refused in violation of the pledges given in the arrangement made and of the act passed at the previous session for her admission. The pretext for this was that her constitution contained a clause directing her legislature to pass laws to prevent free negroes and mulattoes from going to or settling in the state — a provision not to be compared, in its hostility to such persons, to some of the constitutions and laws then and afterward in force in the very states which made this clause the pretext for refusing her admission into the Union. The vote on the resolution for her recognition was ninety-three against, and seventy-two for it. Of these ninety-three, seventy-two were the same men who voted against striking out the state restriction on the *test* vote of the previous session, and seventy-seven of them were the same who voted for the territorial restriction on the 2d of March, 1820. Mr. Clay, as chairman of a committee of thirteen, appointed at his suggestion to settle the difficulty, made a report that Missouri should be recognized as a state in the Union, upon this fundamental condition, that she should pass no law in violation of the constitutional rights of the citizens of the other states; and this resolution, as Mr. Clay said, in 1850, contained merely the declaration of " an incontestable principle of constitutional law." " It is nothing more," he said, " than the principle of the paramount character of the constitution of the United States over any local constitution of any one of the states of the Union." The resolution reported by the committee of thirteen was rejected by a vote of eighty-three to eighty. Mr. Clay, as chairman of a subsequent and much larger committee of the House, appointed in conjunction with a similar one from the Senate, made a report identical in substance with that he had reported as chairman of the committee of thirteen. Nowithstanding this, the resolution passed in the House by a vote of eighty-seven to eighty-one, in the Senate by a vote of twenty-six to fifteen; and on the 10th of August, 1821, the President proclaimed the admission of Missouri into the Union. Of the eighty-seven votes for this last resolution of Mr. Clay for her admission without the slavery restriction, only *seventeen* were from the North; about half of whom were among the fourteen who had voted against the state restriction on the 2d of March, 1820. Of the eighty-one who voted against her admission, eighty were from the North. Are these seventeen anti-restrictionists to represent the party of restrictionists as in favor of the admission of Missouri, rather than the eighty restrictionists as against her admission? Are these seventeen Northern votes to represent the North on this occasion as in favor of the admission of Missouri, or the eighty to represent her as against it? Figures are said not to lie. If so, the truth which these proclaim is that, if the admission of Missouri without the restriction, was the consideration (which it never was) that the North was to pay the South for the Thomas territorial restriction, she certainly never paid it; and therefore her claim on the South to support it was forfeited within twelve months after the compact was made. In addition to the above facts, it may be here stated that those few Northern men, who voted against the restriction on the admission of Missouri, were promptly repudiated by their constituents, who disclaimed being bound by their acts to any political course in the future. This repudiation of their conduct was publicly proclaimed by both legislative and popular action. Indeed, public sentiment was so hostile that in different localities in New England they were burnt in effigy.

But independent of all such matters, the undeniable truth remains, that the only consideration pledged for the admission of Missouri, without the restriction, was the admission of Maine, a proposition so forcibly stated in the words quoted from Mr. Clay, as put by the Senate to the House. That proposition was accepted; the House accordingly, on the 2d of March, 1820, as we have shown, by a majority of three, passed the act for the admission of Missouri, and promptly on the next day, the 3d of March, the Senate receded from its amendments to the Maine bill, which passed it through Congress. The result was, the representatives from Maine applied to Congress at its next session for the recognition of their state as a member of the Union, which was granted; the Senate concurring in fulfillment of its pledge. The representatives from Missouri, as we have seen, made a similar application; but *their* application was rejected by the *House*, in violation of its pledge, and on the pretext we have noticed. Maine, however, let it be said to her praise, completely vindicated her honor through her then noble representatives, in voting and doing all they could for the recognition of Missouri as a state, rightfully in the Union, in fulfillment of a sacred pledge, which they resolved to fulfill, though it had to be done under the fiery indignation of their constituents, and in the light of their own burning effigies.

In 1836, Arkansas applied to Congress for admission into the Union as a slave state. She had a right to be admitted as such, under the Missouri territorial compromise, being a part of the Louisiana territory, south of the line of 36° 30'. The same party of Restrictionists, constituting a majority of those from the North in the House, voted against her admission; denying the obligations of the compromise, or any responsibility whatever, on their part to comply with it. Mr. Adams offered the following amendment to the bill for her admission: "Nothing in this act shall be construed as an assent by Congress to the article of the constitution of the said state in relation to slavery, or the emancipation of slaves, etc."

Mr. Slade, of Vermont, offered also, a restriction against slavery, as an amendment to the bill. Mr. Cushing, of Massachusetts, in discussing the motion of Mr. Adams, alluding to the Missouri compromise, said: "The state of Massachusetts was not a party to that compromise. She never, *directly* or *indirectly*, assented to it; most of her representatives who voted for it, were disavowed and denounced at home." Mr. Hard, of Massachusetts, said: "There was no compromise or compact, whereby Congress surrendered any power;   *   *   if it had done so, it would be subject to repeal at the will of any succeeding Congress, etc." Such was the voice and such the action of Massachusetts and other New England states, in denouncing and repudiating the Missouri compromise on the admission of Arkansas into the Union.

This same party with a like force and unanimity, in 1845, again repudiated the Missouri compromise, when, by an amendment to the resolution, annexing Texas, it was extended by Congress to the territory belonging to that state. They voted against this amendment, notwithstanding the fact that when the Missouri compromise act of 1820 was passed, this same territory was embraced by it as a part of Louisiana; at that time the cession of Texas not having been made to Spain by the Florida treaty.

On the 15th of January, 1847, when a bill for organizing a territorial government for Oregon was pending in the House, to that clause of it which excluded slavery, this amendment was moved: "Inasmuch as the whole of said territory lies north of 36° 30' north latitude, known as the Missouri compromise line." The purpose of this was understood by all, to secure a test vote, to show who were for, and who against the recognition and continuance of that line as a division between the sections, and the amendment was rejected by a vote of one hundred and thirteen to eighty-two. All against it, were from the North, all for it, from the South, except six, of whom Stephen A. Douglas, of Illinois, was the leader. This bill failed to pass the Senate at that session.

After the acquisitions, from Mexico, of California, Utah and New Mexico, another bill for organizing a territorial government for Oregon, with a slavery restriction in it, was passed through the House. When it came before the Senate, Mr. Douglas moved to strike out the restriction, and that the Missouri compromise line be "declared to extend to the Pacific ocean, and be binding for the future organization of the territories of the United States, with the same understanding with which it was orginally adopted." This amendment was passed in the Senate by a vote of thirty-three to twenty-one; twenty-six of the thirty-three were from the South, and all of the twenty-one against it, were from the North. When this amendment came to the House, eighty-two voted for it—all from the South, except four—and one hundred and twenty-one against it, all from the North, except one. Oregon was a part of the Louisiana territory, so claimed in the negotiations with Great Britain, and in the discussions of our title to it in the Senate. The vote, therefore, of the North against the amendment to the first bill was an abrogation of the Missouri compromise, in its application to the very territory which it literally embraced, and in its application to all the other territories, which by its spirit, (as asserted by Mr. Douglas in his amendment), it was intended to embrace.

In view of such a narrative of events, unquestionably true, it appears there is no more indisputable fact recorded, and re-recorded in the annals of Congress and in the history of the country, than that the North, before the year 1850, had wholly abrogated the Missouri compromise, and refused to abide by it, either in its letter or spirit.

This compromise, thus broken and ignored, Mr. Douglas, and those who co-operated with him, no longer regarded as in existence or as a compact to be observed; but looking to another principle in harmony with the Constitution as a substitute for it, he and his fellow Democrats of the North, abandoned his own amendment to the Oregon bill, as a remedy wholly unavailable for settling permanently the slavery question in all the territories as its author had intended. The result was, the Senate receded from it, and the Oregon bill was passed.

The proportion of the common territory allotted between the North and the South, by the Missouri compromise line, as passed in 1821, and proposed in 1848, may be inferred from the following statement. Mr. Kinsey, of New Jersey, one of the conference committee, said in 1820 while addressing the House: "Do our Southern brethren demand an equal division of this wide-spread fertile region (of Louisiana), this common territory, purchased with the common funds of the nation? No, with a magnanimity unparalleled, they have conceded to us *nine-tenths* of this great common property." Mr. Clayton, from Delaware, in 1848, said: "I obtained a statement from the land office. From that statement it appeared that if the (Missouri) line were extended to the Pacific, the free labor of the North would have the exclusive occupation of 1,000,000 square miles and the South, but 262,000."

The compromise of 1850 was the work of Clay, Webster, Douglas and Cass, and most of the great American statesmen of that day. It embraced the admission of California, territorial governments for Utah and New Mexico; the settlement of the question of boundary with Texas; the rendition of fugitive slaves, and the abolition of the slave trade in the District of Columbia. The Missouri compromise having been abrogated, as we have seen, by the North, it was, therefore, considered by these great statesmen as out of the question. Independent of this consideration, Mr. Clay declared the principle of it objectionable, and that it ought not to be adopted. The settlement of the territorial question made in 1850, amounted simply to this: That the principle of restriction by Congress should be entirely abandoned, and that all states hereafter formed, either north, or south of 36° 30', should come into the Union, "either with or without slavery, as their constitutions might prescribe." The bill, said Mr. Clay "has left the field open for both, to be occupied by slavery, if the people, when they are forming states, shall so decide; or to be exclusively devoted to freedom if they shall so determine." The New Mexico bill, as passed, embraced territory obtained from Mexico in 1848, and also territory obtained by the cession of Louisiana in 1803, to which the Missouri compromise had been applied, and which was north of 36° 30'; but this line, having been abandoned now by all parties, was treated as a nullity by this bill, which so far as it came in conflict with the compromise, swept the restriction as a dead letter from the statute book. The vote in the Senate on re-establishing this principle of no Congressional restriction in any of the territories, instead of the principle of division, was thirty-eight for and only twelve against it, twenty *states* for, and six against it. In the House, one hundred and eight for, and ninety-seven against it. This compromise of 1850 was afterwards approved by an overwhelming majority of the people North and South. The Democratic Convention of 1852 endorsed it. The Whig Convention of that year endorsed it, and bound themselves to adhere to it, to use their own language, inserted by Mr. Webster, "*in principle and in substance.*" Mr. Pierce, the Democratic candidate that year, openly and heartily approved it. All the states in the Union, *except four*, voted for him as the chosen advocate of this compromise. For there was nothing of magnetism, either in his personal character or public reputation to attract to him apart from the question at issue, a vote of such magnitude.

In 1854, two delegates appeared at Washington from that portion of the Louisiana cession known as Kansas and Nebraska, with petitions to Congress for territorial governments. Mr. Douglas, as chairman of the Committee on Territories, was instructed to prepare, and report to the Senate, the measures asked for in these petitions. Accordingly, on the 23d of January, 1854, he reported the celebrated Kansas-Nebraska bill, as a substitute for the original Nebraska bill, reported by him on the 4th of January, and identical with the latter, except it divided the territory into two territories, with a government for each, and added a provision for the formal repeal of the Missouri compromise, instead of leaving its repeal to be implied.

In his speech on the Nebraska bill, Mr. Douglas said: "We were aware that, from 1820 to 1850, the abolition doctrine of congressional interference with slavery in the territories and new states, had so far prevailed as to keep up an incessant slavery agitation in Congress, and throughout the country, whenever any new territory was to be acquired or organized. We were also aware, that in 1850 the right of the people to decide this question for themselves, subject only to the constitution, was substituted for the doctrine of congressional intervention. Therefore, the only question in framing this bill was this: Shall we adhere to, and carry out, the principle recognized by the compromise measures of 1850, or shall we go back to the old exploded doctrine of congressional interference, as established in 1820? There were no alternatives. We were compelled to frame the bill upon one or the other of these two principles. The two great political parties of the country stood solemnly pledged before the world to adhere to the compromise measures of 1850, 'in principle and substance.' A large majority of the Senate profess to belong to one or the other of these parties, and, hence, were supposed to be under a high moral obligation to carry out the 'principle and substance' of these measures in all new territorial organizations. The report of the committee is in accordance with this obligation." This report said: "In the judgment of your committee, those measures (of the compromise of 1850) were intended to have a far more comprehensive and enduring effect than the mere adjustment of the difficulties arising out of the recent acquisition of Mexican territory. They were designed to establish certain great principles, which would not only furnish adequate remedies for existing evils, but in all time to come avoid the perils of a similar agitation, by withdrawing the question of slavery from the Halls of Congress, and the political arena, and committing it to the arbitrament of those who were immediately interested in, and alone responsible for, its consequences." "The bill, which your committee have prepared, proposes to carry these propositions and principles into practical operation in the precise language of the compromise measures of 1850." "The legislation of 1850 abrogated the Missouri compromise, so far as the country embraced within the limits of Utah and New Mexico was covered by the slavery restriction. It is true that those acts did not, in terms and by name, repeal the act of 1820, as originally adopted, or as extended by the resolutions annexing Texas in 1845; but the acts of 1850 did authorize the people of those territories to exercise 'all rightful powers of legislation consistent with the constitution,' not excepting the question of slavery; and did provide that when those territories should be admitted into the Union, they should be received with, or without slavery, as the people thereof might determine at the date of their admission. These provisions were in direct conflict with a clause, in any former enactment, declaring that slavery should be forever prohibited in any portion of said territories, and, hence, rendered such clause inoperative and void to the extent of such conflict."

In the 5th clause of the 1st section of the act of 1850, establishing the boundary of Texas, is the following proviso, introduced as an amendment by Mr. Mason, viz.: "Provided, That nothing herein contained shall be construed to impair or qualify anything contained in the 3d article of the 2d section of the 'joint resolution for annexing Texas to the United States,' approved March 1st, 1845; either as regards the number of states that hereafter may be formed out of the state of Texas or otherwise." [The 3d article here referred to is the one also providing for extending the line of 36° 30'.] In his speech of the 3d of March, 1854, Mr. Douglas, commenting on this proviso, said: "The object of this amendment was to guarantee to the state of Texas, with her circumscribed boundaries, the same number of states which she would have had under her larger boundaries, and with the same right to come in, with or without slavery, as they pleased. We have been told, over and over again, that there was no such thing intimated as that the country cut off from Texas was to be relieved from the stipulations of that compromise." Mr. Douglas, after quoting from the debates of 1850 proving this to be false, continues: "It will be seen that the debate goes upon the supposition that the effect was to release the country north of 36° 30' from the obligation of the prohibition, and the only question was whether the declaration that it should be received into the Union, 'with or without slavery,' should be inserted in the Texas bill, or the Territorial bill." *Before* the Kansas-Nebraska bill, in which the clause was inserted, formally repealing the Missouri Compromise act, was reported by Mr. Douglas, Mr. Sumner (who opposed the compromise of 1850), on the 17th of January, 1854, gave notice that he would move an amendment to the original Nebraska bill, reported on the 4th of January (which was in the precise language of the territorial bills of 1850), reaffirming the Missouri compromise of 1820. His amendment was accordingly moved, and ordered to be printed. This was, therefore, the first movement made to abrogate the compromise of 1850, by re-establishing the Missouri compromise, not only in New Mexico, where it had been superseded by another law, but by substituting the principle of it in the place of that established in 1850. This movement not only opened afresh the great issue of 1850, but made the formal repeal of the Missouri compromise in the Kansas-Nebraska bill, reported on the 23d of January, necessary, as a proper replication to the amendment proposed by Mr. Sumner. That amendment would have been as fatal in law to the Territorial act for New Mexico of 1850, so far as there was included in that act Louisiana territory, as it would have been to the Nebraska bill. Who, then, is more responsible for all the agitation of the slavery question, which followed, than Mr. Sumner? On the 19th of January, a manifesto, signed by Mr. Sumner and Mr. Chase, in which they appealed to their friends throughout the country to rally to their support in the agitation of this question, spoke of the Missouri compromise line as the subject of a "sacred pledge," and of a "solemn compact." Just here in point of time, and in the origin of events, is to be found the beginning and the cause from which came, in torrents of passion, that angry contest which rent the nation asunder, drenched our land in blood, and cursed it with all the crimes of civil war. Those who had been known as Restrictionists, soon afterwards, in course of time, became known as Republicans. In their first manifesto, they called that "sacred," which they had uniformly profaned; that a "pledge," which they had never kept; that "solemn," which had been the subject of their sneers; the friends of which, among them, had been hung in mockery and burned in effigy; that a "compact," which, when its very terms required fulfillment, they broke both in letter and spirit.

The Kansas-Nebraska bill passed the House, on the 22d of May, 1854, by a vote of 113 to 100; this majority being greater for the confirmation of the compromise of 1850, including the formal repeal of the Missouri compromise, than for the original act of 1850. By states this vote was eighteen for and thirteen against. In the Senate the bill passed by a vote of thirty-five to thirteen. By states, twenty-one yeas, seven nays, and three divided.

In order to understand more fully the events which followed the passage of this bill, it is well just here to give an extract from a speech made, before it passed, by Mr. Douglas, in the Senate, in which he said: "We have had notice served upon us to-day that the cry of 'repeal' is to resound through the land. * * The Senator from Massachusetts (Mr. Sumner) has told us that the pulpits of New England are to pour forth their denunciations against the execution of an act of Congress for the return of fugitives from service. We are told by that Senator and others that because we repeal a law, which has been upon the statute book since 1820, and has been inoperative during the whole period for the reason that there were no people upon whom it could operate, they regard themselves as released from the obligations resting upon them to support the Constitution, and from their oaths to observe its injunctions. Men here who occupy seats only by virtue of an oath to preserve the Constitution, tell us that, because of the passage of this law, they will commit perjury, they will violate the Constitution, they will repudiate their oaths, they will defy God and man, in resistance to the constitution and the law of the land. Sir, the Senator from Massachusetts has told us to-night that these protesting clergymen from New England will engage in that work of perfidy, and perjury, and treason against the Constitution." On the 12th of March, 1856, Mr. Douglas, from the Committee on Territories, submitted a report to the Senate, in which the following passages occur: " Finding opposition to the principles of the Kansas-Nebraska act unavailing in the Halls of Congress, and under the forms of the constitution, combinations were immediately entered into, in some portions of the Union, to control the political destinies, and form and regulate the domestic institutions of those territories and future states, through the machinery of Emigrant aid societies. In order to give consistency and efficiency to the movement, and surround it with the color of legal authority, an act of incorporation was procured from the Legislature of Massachusetts, in which it was provided in the first section that twenty persons therein named, and their 'associates, successors and assigns, are hereby made a corporation, by the name of the Massachusetts Emigrant Aid Company, for the purpose of assisting emigrants to settle in the West.' The committee here enter into a detail of the Massachusetts society, and remark: "When a powerful corporation, with a capital of five millions of dollars invested in houses and lands, in merchandise and mills, in cannon and rifles, in powder and lead, in all the implements of art, agriculture, and war, and employing a corresponding number of men, all under the control and management of non-resident directors and stockholders, who are authorized by their charter to vote by proxy to the extent of fifty votes each, enters a distant and sparsely-settled territory with the fixed purpose of wielding all its power to control the domestic institutions and political doctrines of the territory, it becomes a question of fearful import how far the operations of the company are compatible with the rights and liberties of the people." * * "Exaggerated accounts of the large number of emigrants on their way, under the auspices of the Emigrant aid companies, with the view of controling the election for members of the territorial legislature, which was to take place on the 30th of March, 1855, were published and circulated. These accounts, being republished and believed in Missouri, where the excitement had already been inflamed to a fearful intensity, induced a corresponding effort to send at least an equal number to counteract the apprehended result of this new importation." Thus, these political agitators of the slavery question, such as Sumner, Seward and Chase, after their signal defeat in the national councils in 1850 and 1854, sought by Emigrant aid societies to extend this sectional conflict from the halls of Congress to the plains of Kansas; and by 'Personal Liberty bills', and unlawful combinations in the several states, to resist successfully the fugitive slave law; all of which culminated in 1856 in the formation of the Republican party, with John C. Fremont as their candidate for President. Mr. Buchanan received the nomination of the Democratic party for the same office; which he accepted with its platform endorsing, in words of unqualified approval, the Kansas-Nebraska act of 1854. He carried nineteen states, and Col. Fremont only eleven. Maryland voted for Mr. Fillmore. The popular vote for Col. Fremont was 1,341,264; while the whole vote against him was 2,802,703. Mr. Buchanan's electoral majority over both his opponents was sixty. Thus the Kansas-Nebraska act, with its repeal of the Missouri compromise, was, by an overwhelming popular and electoral majority of the nation, approved.

In addition to the above historical facts, the very question at issue in regard to the territories came up before the Supreme Court of the United States, in the celebrated Dred-Scott case. This case having been determined by the Supreme Court of Missouri, in 1852, adversely to Dred Scott, and remanded to the court below, his counsel endeavored to better his client's chances by resorting to another jurisdiction, and accordingly carried the case into the Federal Court, at St. Louis, on the 2d of November, 1853, where it was decided, and by writ of error taken to the Supreme Court of the United States *before* the Kansas-Nebraska bill was passed After the case had been heard twice, and after the most deliberate consideration and elaborate research by each and all of the Judges, Chief Justice TANEY, in 1857, delivered the opinion of the court, deciding in clear, unequivocal language, the question as above stated against the Republican party, and in favor of the constitutional right as exercised under the earliest administrations of the Government, as maintained by Jefferson and Madison, and as claimed by the South. The Judges of this august tribunal had been appointed to their offices, from different sections of the Union, before the existence of the Republican party, and before its issues had been formed. Unlike the appointment by a late Republican President of two Judges to the Supreme Bench, for the purpose of getting a party decision, and for party ends, these Judges were free from any such committals to a preconcerted judgment, were wholly independent, and above all party dictation, of unblemished character, and of the highest judicial integrity. The decision, therefore, deserved to be received by all fair-minded men as an honest and impartial one, free from any possible reproach, or impeachment as to its integrity of purpose, and high judicial character. Mr. Lincoln, in his canvass with Mr. Douglas, speaking of the above decision, said: "If the territories attempt, by any direct legislation, to drive the man with his slave out of the territory, or to decide that his slave is free because of his being taken in there, or to tax him to such an extent that he cannot keep him there, the Supreme Court will unhesitatingly decide all such legislation unconstitutional, as long as that Supreme Court is constructed as the Dred Scott's

Supreme Court is. The first two things *they have* already *decided*, except that there is a *little quibble* among lawyers between the words dicta and decision." "Judge Douglas understands the constitution according to the Dred Scott decision, and he is bound to support it (the constitution) as he understands it. *I* understand it *another way*, and, therefore, I am bound to support it in the *way* in *which I understand it.*" Here, let it be observed, Mr. Lincoln very justly recognizes the truth that the territorial question was judicially before the court for its decision, and that all objection to it as mere *dicta* was no more than a lawyer's *quibble;* and that the ground of his disobedience to it was, that he differed with the court in his construction of the constitution. He further said: " If I were in Congress, and a vote should come up on a question whether slavery should be prohibited in a new territory, *in spite* of the Dred Scott decision, I would vote that *it should.*" So the Republican party declared that they would not be bound by this decision nor by the precedents and practice of the government under Washington, Adams, Jefferson, and Madison, but that they would give *their own construction* to the constitution and enforce it. Let us now turn our attention to the second right claimed by the South.

From the days of Washington to the election of Lincoln, Congress, in acting on the clause in the constitution for the return of fugitives from service, had passed laws for its faithful fulfillment in the reclamation of runaway slaves. Congress, in 1793, with the approval of Washington, had passed an act for carrying this provision into effect, which had been approved by the Supreme Court as constitutional, and which had been executed without interference through the administrations of the Fathers of the Declaration of Independence and of the constitution, and until the years from 1840 to 1850. Within this decade, the elements of the future Republican party sprang into existence, and began to be formed into an organized opposition, one purpose of which was to resist the enforcement of the above constitutional provision through the action of state authority. To counteract this organized and rebellious effort, the act of 1850 was passed; in the advocacy of which Mr. Webster declared: "That there has been found at the North, among individuals and among legislators, a disinclination to perform fully their constitutional duties in regard to the return of persons, bound to service, who have escaped into the free states. In that respect, the South, in my judgment, is right, and the North is wrong. Every member of every Northern legislature is bound by oath, like every other officer of the country, to support the constitution, which says to these states that they shall deliver up fugitives from service, which is as binding in honor and conscience as any other article. No man fulfills his duty, in any legislature, who sets himself to excuses, evasions, escapes from this constitutional obligation. I put it to all the sober, sound minds at the North, as a question of morals and a question of conscience. What right have they, in their legislative capacity, or *any other capacity*, to endeavor to get round this constitution, or to embarrass the *free exercise* of the rights secured by the constitution to the persons whose fugitives escape from them? None at all. None at all; neither in the forum of conscience, nor before the face of the constitution, are they, in my opinion, justified in such an attempt. I repeat, therefore, sir, that there is a well-founded ground of complaint against the North which ought to be removed; which calls for the enactment of proper laws authorizing the judicature of this government, in the several states, to do all that is necessary for the recapture of fugitives, and for the restoration to those who claim them." In confirmation and support of the truth of these admissions by the North, through her most distinguished representative, the act of 1850, amendatory of that of 1793, was passed by Congress, approved by all the departments of the Government, declared to be constitutional by its judiciary, and sought to be enforced by its judgments and processes. It was also one of those compromise measures of 1850, framed by Clay, Webster, and Douglas, which, in the election of Mr. Pierce, had been so signally approved by an overwhelming majority of the American people, both North and South. Mr. Lincoln, in his speech at Jonesboro, in 1858, said: "I recollect I, as a member of that (the Whig) party, *acquiesced* in that compromise. All had acquiesced in the compromise measures of 1850. We never had been seriously disturbed by any abolition agitation before that period." Finally, however, so far from securing the return of fugitives, in fulfillment of a plain provision of the constitution, this act aroused and strengthened the resistance to it; so that states in the North endeavored, through their state legislatures and courts, to defeat its enforcement under the assertion of a false doctrine of state rights and state sovereignty. The acts here alluded to were passed under the name of "Personal Liberty Bills." To illustrate their true character, let us cite the act of Vermont, in which it was provided, that such persons, as are called fugitives from service or labor, " who shall come," or " shall be in this state, shall be *free*;" and then provides that any person who shall hold or attempt to hold one in violation of such freedom, " shall, on conviction thereof, be imprisoned in the state prison for a term not less than five years nor more than twenty, and be fined not less than $1,000." Thus did this act not only intend, but *professed*, to nullify a federal law, and a provision of the constitution itself.

In 1856, a party of fugitives escaped from Kentucky into Ohio. A warrant for their apprehension was obtained from one Pendery, a Federal Commissioner appointed by Judge McLean, of the Supreme Court of the United States, under the fugitive slave act of 1850. This warrant was executed by a United States Marshal, who placed the fugitives in custody. The opponents of the law then procured a writ of *habeas corpus*, returnable before a State Probate Judge, named Burgoyne, which the sheriff executed so far as to take into his custody the fugitives, and lodge them in the county jail. Judge Leavitt, of the United States Court, before whom the case was brought, announced his decision, and declared that the custody of the sheriff as against the claim of the Marshal under the fugitive act, was unlawful, and ordered the former to deliver the fugitives to the latter. In the meantime Burgoyne, the Probate Judge, hastened to Columbus to see Governor Chase, to know of him, if he would sustain the process of the State Probate Court, against the proceedings of the General Government for the delivering up of the fugitives under the act of 1850. Governor Chase, who has given a narrative himself of the above facts, states his reply to the application made to him, as the Executive of Ohio in these words: " I did not hesitate to assure him (Burgoyne, the Probate Judge), that the process of the *State* Courts should be enforced in every part of the State, whether in Hamilton, or any other county, and *authorized him* to say *to the sheriff*, that in the performance of his duties he would be sustained by the whole power at the command of the Executive." Before this authority reached the sheriff he had obeyed the order of Judge Leavitt, and the resistance, or rather open rebellion, not only threatened, but ordered by the *Republican* Governor of Ohio against the action of the General Government was thus averted. Referring afterwards to this case, Mr. Chase, on the 13th of March, 1864, wrote to Mr. Trowbridge as follows: "All that I could do in their (the fugitives') behalf, under the circumstances then existing, was done; the power of the State was pledged to maintain the process of the State." Gov. Chase, in a letter to the South, dated at Columbus, November 30, 1860, wrote as follows: "Besides the question of extension, there seems to me to be but one other which need occasion any anxiety. I refer, of course, to the extradition of escaping slaves. I have no doubt that the constitution stipulates for such extradition of escaping slaves; but I cannot help saying the natural sentiment and conscientious convictions make the execution of this stipulation, in the free states, well nigh impracticable, and I would not delude, or attempt to delude, any body with the notion of its execution under what some people call '*a fair law*;' for all such propositions *mean evasion*, and I would evade nothing. It is high time to have done with evasion. In this spirit I would recognize *the fact* of *constitutional obligation*, and the fact that *it cannot be fulfilled* with any thing like completeness."

In the Peace Congress, in February, 1861, Gov. Chase, just before entering Mr. Lincoln's Cabinet, spoke as follows: "I must speak to you plainly, gentlemen of the South. It is not in my heart to deceive you. I therefore tell you explicitly, that if we of the North and West would consent to throw away all that has been gained in the recent triumph of our principles, the people would not sustain us, and so the consent would avail you nothing. And I must tell you further that under no inducements whatever will we consent to surrender a principle which we believe to be so sound and so important as that of restricting slavery within state limits." "Aside from (this) the territorial question, I know of but one serious difficulty. I refer to the question concerning fugitives from service. The people of the free states, however, who believe that slave-holding is wrong, cannot and will not aid in the reclamation; and the *stipulation* (in the constitution) *becomes, therefore, a dead letter*. You complain of bad faith, and the complaint is retorted by denunciations of the cruelty which would drag back to bondage the poor slave who has escaped from it." On the 4th of March, 1861, a few days after the delivery of this open and unreserved confession by Mr. Chase, that the Republican party of the North had refused, and would continue to refuse, to permit the fugitive slave clause of the Constitution to be enforced, Mr. Lincoln, in his inaugural, confessed the truth of the statements of his distinguished cabinet officer, by referring to what he called "the fugitive slave clause" of the Constitution in these words: "The moral sense of the people (of the North) imperfectly supports the law itself," and "fugitive slaves are only partially surrendered;" acknowledging thus the constitution to be broken. With a conscious distrust of getting what he asked for, he appealed to his party to make good the oath, which he admitted they had violated, in the following words: "All members of Congress swear their support to the *whole* Constitution; to this provision as well as to any other. To the proposition, then, that slaves, whose cases come within the terms of this clause (quoting from the Constitution, '*shall* be *delivered up*,' their *oaths* are unanimous. Now *if they would make the effort* in *good temper*, could they not with nearly equal unanimity frame and pass a law, by means of which to keep good that unanimous oath?" In his debate with Douglas he had said: "Why do I yield support to a fugitive slave law? Because I do not understand the Constitution which guarantees that right can be supported without it." He also uses the following bitter and scathing language towards those who would favor hostile legislation against a man's recognized constitutional right to hold his slave, of which there is no stronger illustration than the enactments of the 'Personal Liberty Bills.'" "Can he (a member of a legislature) withhold the legislation, which his neighbor needs for the enjoyment of a right which is fixed in his favor in the Constitution of the United States, which he has sworn to support? Can he withhold it without violating his oath? and more especially can he pass unfriendly legislation to violate his oath? Why, this is a *monstrous* sort of talk about the Constitution of the United States! There has never been as *outlandish or lawless a doctrine from the mouth of any respectable man on earth.*" Hopeless, therefore, as Mr. Lincoln evidently considered it to enforce the fugitive slave clause of the Constitution in the North, he held that every federal and state officer, every member of Congress and of a state legislature, every judicial and executive officer was bound, in swearing to support the Constitution, to support that clause as well as any other; and, therefore, when they sought to evade, or defeat it, by any act either federal or state, they were guilty of perjury. Commenting on the same clause, Mr. Webster, at Capon Springs, Virginia, in

1851, addressing the South, said: " How absurd it is to suppose, that when different parties enter into a compact for certain purposes, either can disregard any one provision, and expect nevertheless the other to observe the rest? I have not hesitated to say, and I repeat, that if the Northern states refuse wilfully and deliberately to carry into effect that part of the Constitution which respects the restoration of fugitive slaves, and Congress provide no remedy, the South would no longer be bound to observe the compact. A bargain cannot be broken on one side, and still bind the other side. I say to you, gentlemen in Virginia, as I said on the shores of lake Erie and in the city of Boston, as I may say again in that city, or elsewhere in the North, that you of the South have as much right to receive your fugitive slaves, as the North has to any of its rights and privileges of navigation and commerce."

In the case of *Prigg* v. *Pennsylvania*, Justice STORY, of Massachusetts, in delivering the opinion of the Supreme Court, and referring to the restoration of fugitive slaves, said: " The full recognition of this right and title was indispensable to the security of this species of property in all the slave-holding states, and indeed was so *vital* to the preservation of their domestic interests and institutions, that it cannot be doubted that it constituted a *fundamental* article, without the adoption of which the Union could not have been formed. The clause was, therefore, of the *last importance* to the safety and security of the Southern states. The clause was accordingly adopted into the Constitution by the *unanimous* consent of the framers of it; a proof at once of its intrinsic and practical necessity. We have not the slightest hesitation in holding that, under and by virtue of the Constitution, the owner of a slave is clothed with entire authority, in every state in the Union, to seize and recapture his slave, whenever he can do it without any breach of the peace, or any illegal violence. In this sense, and to this extent, this clause of the Constitution may properly be said to *execute itself.*" From the foregoing statement and discussion, the following conclusions are undeniable, viz., That in 1860 the Republican party assumed these two positions: *First.* That they would, by an act of Congress, exclude the Southerners with their slaves from *all* the common territories which belonged, or thereafter might belong, to the United States; and this they would do, without a precedent in the history of the Government, in opposition to the recorded opinions of Jefferson and Madison, in 1819 and 1820, in their letters to Walsh, Monroe, and Holmes, against its constitutionality; in opposition to the principle of the Missouri compromise; to the compromise of 1850; to the Kansas-Nebraska bill of 1854; and in violation of a most deliberate and able decision of the Supreme Court of the nation, pronouncing such an act unconstitutional, sustaining the opinions of Jefferson and Madison against restriction, and confirming the principles of the compromise of 1850. *Second.* That they would not permit the enforcement of the fugitive slave clause of the Constitution. It was "*a dead letter.*" This they declared, notwithstanding the Supreme Court, in *Prigg* v. *Pennsylvania*, decided that it was "*vital*" to the interests of the South, and "a *fundamental* article," which had been unanimously adopted because of its absolute necessity. Notwithstanding Mr. Lincoln, in his inaugural, from a sense of conscious duty, in defiance of his own party in Congress, advocated the execution of the fugitive slave clause, and told them their oaths "were unanimous" to its fulfillment, and elsewhere declared that any *unfriendly* legislation against a constitutional right to hold a slave was "*monstrous;*" and was an "*outlandish*" and "*lawless doctrine*" from the mouth of *any respectable man.*" So strongly was *he* in favor of an efficient fugitive slave law, that in his speech at Ottawa he publicly said: " I would give them (the Southern people) any legislation for the reclaiming of their fugitives, which should not in its stringency be more likely to carry a free man into slavery, than our ordinary criminal laws are to hang an innocent one!"

In disregard of these strong utterances of Mr. Lincoln for the execution of the fugitive slave clause, charging perjury against those who failed to support it; in defiance of the decision of the Supreme Court that it was "fundamental" and "vital" to the interests of the South; the Republican party in effect declared, through Mr. Chase and others of equal authority, that all their officers throughout the federal and state governments, although sworn to support the clause, would violate it rather than offend their *moral sense* in executing it.

Again, the Republican party declared they would prohibit the Southerners from going with their slave property into any common territory of the United States, in opposition to all precedents in the administration of the Government, in violation of the Constitution as construed by Jefferson and Madison, the highest authorities known to American history, and as expounded by the decision of the Supreme Court of the Union, pronounced on the very question at issue.

These were the positions of the Republican party, on the ground of which the South rebelled and determined to separate.

To have resorted to this dire alternative of dissolving a Union, hallowed by all the blood of the Revolution, and all the blessings it had bestowed, rather than trusted the gallant Democracy of the North, to have restored *within the Union*, the Constitution as construed by the Fathers, and triumphantly maintained by the nation in '52, '54 and '56 *against* the positions of the Republican party, which in '60, for the first time, had won by the mere forms of the Constitution its "brief authority," with a popular majority of near a million, and a majority of Congress and of the Supreme Court *against them*. How great the folly! how unwise the act! how egregious the error! can alone be told by all the blood and treasure shed and lost, by all the disasters, cruelties and crimes of the civil war which followed.

Prior to the war the Democracy of the North under the leadership of such men as Seymour, Douglas, Hendricks and Pendleton, had opposed the course of the Republican party in its flagrant violations of the Constitution and of their oaths to support it. But war modifies the relations of political parties to each other and to those entrusted with the Government and its preservation through the perils and dangers of the conflict. Party strifes and discords which tend to weaken the military arm and force of the Government, should be suspended as far as possible for the time, and all the powers of a united people concentrated in the effort to save the country and achieve a victory over the common foe. In conformity with this high and patriotic duty the Democracy of the North acted throughout the conflict.

In the first year of the war, Congress by an unanimous vote in the Senate, and with but two negative votes in the House, passed a resolution solemnly declaring the only objects and purposes for which the war then existing was to be prosecuted. It was declared to be: "Not for any purpose of conquest, or subjugation, nor for the purpose of overthrowing, or interfering with, the rights or established institutions of those states, but to defend and maintain the supremacy of the Constitution, and all laws made in pursuance thereof, and to preserve the Union, with all the dignity, equality, and rights of the several states unimpaired." Mr. Lincoln, in December, 1864, stated to Congress, and on the 3d of February, 1865, to the Commissioners of the Confederacy, " the abandonment of armed resistance to the National authority, on the part of the insurgents, as the only indispensable condition of ending the war on the part of the government;" and to make his meaning still more explicit, he added: " In stating a *single condition of peace*, I mean simply to say, that the war *will cease on the part of the government, whenever it shall have ceased on the part of those who began it.*" The conditions of Lee's surrender to Grant, on the 9th of April, 1865, were in substance: *First,* That the officers and men under the former were not to take up arms against the government; and, *Secondly,* that, on surrendering their arms, they were " allowed to return home, and were not to be disturbed by the United States authority so long as they observe the laws in force where they may reside." By virtue of these terms of peace, (the same in substance proposed by Mr. Lincoln to the Confederate Commissioners) and by virtue of the pledge of the government to the people of the Union who supported the war, that it should be prosecuted only to " maintain the Supremacy of the Constitution," and " to preserve the Union," " with all the *equality* and rights of the several states unimpaired," the Southern States, on their submission, were *de jure* entitled to their equal rights under the Constitution. Before they came, however, practically into the enjoyment of those rights, there were three amendments to the Constitution submitted to them, which were adopted under the forms required by its amendatory clause, and which were in substance as follows:

First, The abolition of slavery was provided for.

Second, It was provided that all persons born in the United States, or naturalized, and subject to its jurisdiction, should be citizens thereof, and of the state where they reside.

Third, That the right of citizens of the United States to vote shall not be denied, or abridged by the United States, or by any state, on account of race, color or previous condition of servitude. By this provision no right of suffrage is given; that is left to come alone from the states.

Such, in brief, were the three amendments. And in order that the after professions of parties shall be corrected by the events themselves to which they relate—it may be well just here to observe, that the Republican Party, from the commencement to the end of the war, declared that the abolition of slavery in the South was no object of its prosecution. The step which Mr. Lincoln took, as its leader, towards that end, by his proclamation during the war, was apologized for by him and his party as an act, forced upon them, of self-defense; a "mere war measure," designed in its use like the destruction of any other means of strength to the enemy, only to cripple and defeat him. It was *disavowed* as a measure of philanthropy, or good will, claimed for the benefit of the colored man; but merely that he might be made an instrument of triumph over a dangerous foe. Mr. Lincoln, the President and leader of the Republican Party, in 1864, wrote: "I aver that to this day I have done *no official act* in mere deference to any abstract *judgment and feeling on slavery.*" "When early in the war, Gen. Fremont attempted military emancipation, I forbade it, because I did not then *think it an indispensable necessity.* When a little later Gen. Cameron suggested the arming of the blacks, I objected, because I did not yet think it an indispensable necessity. When still later Gen. Hunter attempted military emancipation, I again forbade it, because I did not think the *indispensable necessity* had come. I was, in my best judgment, *driven* to the alternative of either surrendering the Union, and with it the Constitution, or of laying the strong hand on the colored element. I chose the latter. My enemies pretend I am now carrying on this war for the sole purpose of abolition. So long as I am President, it shall be carried on for the *sole purpose* of restoring the Union. But *no human power* can subdue this Rebellion without the use of the emancipation policy. Let my enemies prove to the country that the destruction of slavery is not necessary to the restoration of the Union. I will abide the issue." The Republican Party, therefore, only sought the liberty of the slave, that he might, in slaying his master, save his liberator.

After Mr. Lincoln's proclamation, serious apprehensions were felt that those negroes freed by it might come North. Petitions from the people against it were sent to Northern Legislatures. A few extracts from the reports in response to them by Republican Committees will show that it was not on account of any partiality for the negro which induced the Republicans to seek his freedom.

One of those reports declares: "If slaves are discharged from bondage, and made free by the proclamation, it will only make the South a congenial place for the negro race; such an event would not only make the South more desirable for those already there, but it would be a strong invitation for those in the Northern States to take up their abode in that climate. We do not, therefore, deem it necessary to take any action upon the subject. If there was real *danger* of a great influx of negroes into the state, we admit it would merit a more serious consideration. We think, however, that the assumption that such danger exists at the present time, is not well founded." Another report from a committee of the Legislature of Wisconsin, signed exclusively by Republicans, said: "Since the Federal Government has been forced into the emancipation war policy, the inducement from such persons (the negroes) to come North has been removed, and instead of colored laborers coming to the North, it will take most of them *out of the North*. The colored man is *an animal* of the tropics; is as much out of place in even a temperate zone, as a polar bear would be in the jungles of Bengal. While the blackman keeps the place assigned him, he would be treated with more consideration in the South, than in the North. In the North, the black man has no place assigned him in society. Will they (the black men) leave a society where, at least, they would be tolerated, for one where *they are despised?*" "What I would most desire," said Mr. Lincoln, "would be the separation of the white and black races."

The Fifteenth Amendment was no object of the war. Nor was it for any partiality to the freedmen of the colored race that the Republicans sought to enfranchise them in the South, but merely thereby to enlarge and perpetuate in power their own party. For in states of the North, where Republican rule prevailed, the enfranchisement of the colored man, and the ordinary political and civil rights of citizenship, had been long denied him. Let us illustrate this by a few facts.

In 1833, Miss Crandall, a well educated lady who had an excellent boarding school for girls in Canterbury, Conn., received a bright young colored woman of fine character as a pupil. When the parents of some of the white scholars threatened to remove their children if the "nigger girl" was permitted to remain, and Miss Crandall saw that she could no longer expect to have a full school from that neighborhood, she gave notice in Canterbury that her school would be opened for young ladies of color. This excited the fiercest wrath of the community. She had been grossly insulted and threatened, and a town meeting was held to adopt such measures as would effectually avert the nuisance. To this meeting a multitude came from the neighboring towns. Strong resolutions were offered and abusive speeches were made by men of prominence, and when Miss Crandall, by a note to the chairman, asked that Messrs May and Buffum might be heard in her defense, fists were doubled in their faces and they were not permitted to speak. The school opened with fifteen or twenty colored girls from different parts of the country. But no storekeeper, or dealer in provisions, in the town, would furnish the needful supplies. Miss Crandall and her pupils were insulted in the street; the doors and door-steps of her house were besmeared, and her well was filled with filth. On the 24th of May, 1833, the Legislature of Connecticut enacted a law (for the occasion) known as the "black law." It provided under heavy penalties, "that no school should be established in any town of the State for the education of colored persons of other towns, without the consent in writing, first obtained, of a majority of the civil authority and the select men of the town." At Miss Crandall's first trial, the jury did not agree. A new indictment was hastily drawn and a verdict was given against her. Miss Crandall's house was set on fire, but by timely exertion was saved from destruction. At about midnight of the 9th of September, the house was assaulted by a band of persons with heavy clubs and iron bars, who broke in and destroyed windows, rendering a portion of the house quite untenantable. (See Life of Rev. Samuel J. May by George B. Emerson and others). "After due consideration, therefore," says Mr. May in his Recollections, "it was determined that the school should be abandoned. Never before had I felt so deeply sensible of the cruelty of the persecution which had been carried on for eighteen months, in that New England village, against a family of defenseless females." "Twenty harmless, well behaved girls, whose only offence against the peace of the commonwealth was, that they had come together there to obtain useful knowledge and moral culture, were to be told that they must go away." The Rev. Samuel J. May was a distinguished anti-slavery man and author, of Boston birth, whose mother was the neice of the wife of John Hancock, and whose works have been the subject of eulogy by Sparks, Bancroft, and Everett.

By the seventh section of a law of Massachusetts of 1786, which remained in force until 1843, it was provided "that no person shall join in marriage any white person with any negro, or mulatto, under penalty of £50, and all such marriages shall be absolutely null and void," making necessarily those born in such a wedlock *bastards*. By a law of the same State of 1788, unrepealed until 1834, it was provided that no person being an African or negro, other than a subject of Morocco, or a citizen of some one of the United States (to be evidenced by a certificate from the Secretary of the State of which he shall be a citizen), shall tarry within this commonwealth for a longer time than two months; and upon complaint made to any Justice of the Peace within this commonwealth, that any such person has been within the same more than two months, the said Justice shall order the said person to depart out of this commonwealth; and in case that the said African or negro shall not depart as aforesaid, any Justice, upon complaint and proof made that such person has continued within this commonwealth ten days after notice given, shall commit the said person to any house of correction within the county, to be kept to *hard labor*, etc.," and if such person continued to remain it was provided "he or she shall be whipped, not exceeding ten stripes, and ordered to depart within ten days." This process of punishment could be renewed every two months. To what extent this law was enforced against individual persons and single families of the colored race in Massachusetts, through the period of its existence for near fifty years, passing as it did the approval of several revisions of the Statutes, can never be established now, for the want of published and preserved records in such cases; but one memorable and signal enforcement occurred, of which there is ample proof. In the Massachusetts *Mercury*, of Boston, dated Sept. 16, 1800, No. 22, Vol. 16, is a notice to blacks, stating that the Officers of Police having made returns under the above law to the Subscriber, Charles Bulfinch, Superintendent, of certain persons, Africans or negroes, whose names are given, "the same are hereby warned and directed to depart out of this commonwealth before the 10th of October next, as they would avoid the pains and penalties of the law," etc. The names of these colored men and women then follow to the number of *239*, whose former residences in other counties are named; some from Rhode Island, New York, Philadelphia, Liverpool, France, etc. Without the list of names the above notice is also to be found in the *Commercial Advertiser* of the 20th, and the *Daily Advertiser* of the 22d of September, 1800, both of New York, and in other papers. Mr. Nell, in his work on the Colored Patriots of the American Revolution, notices an African Benevolent Society, instituted in Boston, in 1796. He says its benevolent objects were set forth in the preamble which also expressed its loyalty as follows: "Behaving ourselves at the same time as true and faithful citizens of the commonwealth in which we live, and that we take no one into the Society who shall commit any injustice or outrage against the laws of their country." He adds a list of the members of the African Society. A comparison of this list with that in the above notice shows one-fourth of the members were driven out of the commonwealth in 1800. Except Massachusetts, it is believed, no civilized, free or slave state in christendom ever stained its statute books with so barbarous and inhuman a law, by which color was not only made a crime, but free men and free women were banished from their homes where they had lived before the law was passed.

When the Illinois Constitution of 1848 was framed, there were two provisions in it which were separately submitted to the people for their adoption or rejection. One was, that no negro or mulatto shall be permitted to migrate or settle in the state; on this, the vote was 171,896 to 71,806, being a majority of 100,590 for the provision against the admission of negroes into Illinois. The other was that they should not hold office, or have the right of suffrage; on this, the vote was 211,920 to 35,649, being a majority of 176,271 against allowing the negroes to hold office or to vote in Illinois. To carry these provisions into effect, an act was passed in 1853, which provided, that: "If a negro or mulatto, bond or free, shall, hereafter, come into this state, and remain ten days with the evident intention of residing in the same; every such negro or mulatto, shall be deemed guilty of a high misdemeanor, and for the first offense, shall be fined the sum of fifty dollars. If such negro or mulatto shall be found guilty, and the fine assessed be not paid, *forthwith*, to the Justice of the Peace before whom the proceedings were had, it shall be the duty of said justice to commit said negro, or mulatto, to the custody of the sheriff, or otherwise keep him, her or them, in custody; and said justice shall forthwith advertise said negro, or mulatto, and on the day and at the time and place; mentioned in said advertisement, the said justice shall, at public auction, proceed to sell said negro or mulatto, to any person, or persons, who will pay said fine and costs for the shortest time; and said purchaser shall have the right to compel said negro or mulatto to work for, and serve out said time. If said negro, or mulatto, shall not within ten days after the expiration of his, her or their time of service, as aforesaid, leave the state, he, she, or they shall be liable to a second prosecution, in which the penalty to be inflicted, shall be one hundred dollars, and so on for every subsequent offense, the penalty shall be increased fifty dollars, over and above the last penalty." This act came from a Judiciary Committee of the Legislature of Illinois, Mr. Lincoln's own state, in 1853; and was not repealed until 1865! It was reported from the above named committee by John A. Logan, the present Republican Senator of Illinois, who was the father and champion of it, and who, as the record shows, carefully guarded its severe and cruel provisions against all amendments offered and pressed for adoption. Mr. Lincoln's sentiments, however, as the great leader and spokesman of the Republican party, were in harmony with the object of this law. It is not known that he ever suggested a modification of it during his whole political career before the war, but on the contrary he said: "I am not, nor ever have been, in favor of bringing about *in any way* the social and political equality of the white and black races. I am not, nor ever have been, in favor of *making voters of the free negroes*, or *jurors*, or qualifying them *to hold office*, or having them to marry with white people. I will say in addition, that there is a *physical difference* between the white and black races, which I suppose will forever forbid the two races living together upon terms of social and political equality, and inasmuch as they cannot so live, that while they do remain together, there *must be* the superior and inferior, *I, as much as any other man*, am in favor of the superior being assigned to the white man." "They the Southern people, are just what we would be in their situation. If slavery did not exist among them, they would *not introduce it*. If it did now exist amongst us, *we* should not instantly give it up. When Southern people tell us they are no more responsible for the origin of slavery than we, I acknowledge the facts. That it is very difficult to get rid of it, in any satisfactory way, I can understand, and appreciate the saying, I surely will not blame them for not doing what I should not know how to do myself. If all earthly power were given me, I should not know what to do as to the existing institution. My first impulse would be to free all the slaves and *send them to Liberia.*" Thus Mr. Lincoln asserted the great superiority of his own race over that of the negro, which, in the freedom of the latter, he held, should ever be observed in the distinctions of society, and in the administration of our Government. He believed that in the same society, and under the same government, you could no more elevate the one race to the line of equality, without degrading the other, than you could make black white. While his hand was forced to pen the proclamation of freedom for the African, to save those of his own race from ruin, his prayer still was, "Shield me and mine from that philanthropy which would blend the crystal eye, the elevated feature, the ambrosial and waving curl, the rosy skin, all the striking and glorious attributes that mark the favorites of nature, exhaling fragrance and redolent of beauty and of bloom, with the disgusting peculiarities, the wool and grease and fetor of the blackened savage of the southern deserts. The Saxon and the Celt, the Norman and the Dane, even the Tartar and the Hun, the Turk and Saracen, the races of Japhet and of Shem, may compound and melt and mingle into one people, when met upon the same soil; but the race of Ham must serve or separate." Such was the language of one who thought and felt with Mr. Lincoln, on the subject of the position in which the freed or free-born African should stand related to the white man under the same government. It surely was one of subjection, if not of bondage; one of servitude if not of slavery. For what else is *he*, though called a freeman, but a *servant*, who, according to the only *Magna Charta* granted him, is to be taxed without representation, governed without his consent, excluded from office, tried without a jury of his peers, and forbidden to marry in any race but his own? Such was the only colored freeman allowed to remain in this country by the political creed of Mr. Lincoln in 1860, the great Republican leader and apostle of human liberty.

The same man, and the same Republican party, in their platform of 1860, denounced John Brown for his raid upon Virginia to rescue the slave from his master, as among the worst of criminals. So, too, they pledged themselves at the commencement of the war, by a resolution passed by Congress with but two dissenting votes, that they would not prosecute it for any purpose of freeing the slave; and declared during its progress to the end of it, through Mr. Lincoln, that the pledge had been kept, and that no slave had been freed except from necessity to save the white man and his government.

The terms of surrender were agreed upon, by which both parties resumed their positions in a state of peace, under the Constitution and the laws made in pursuance thereof. The laws of war, with their rigid rights and rules, no longer existed. That which war gave authority to do, peace now made illegal and void. Neither the people nor States of the South could now be treated as rebels or belligerents, for the simple reason that they were now in fact neither; the admission and recognition of which formed necessarily the very basis of the terms of peace. By that agreement no penalties were inflicted, or provided for; no rights under the Constitution were withheld by the victors from the vanquished; but on the contrary the latter, by the very terms of surrender, were bound to obey the Constitution, and therefore to aid in the execution of all its rights and obligations. The Republican party, in utter disregard of these terms, and of the Constitution, and of the pledges given in the resolution passed so unanimously by Congress at the commencement of the war, placed the Southern people and States under military law, treating them as captives of war and conquered provinces. This they did for party ends and purposes, but under a false profession that it was done to protect a race whose rights as freemen they had shamefully ignored and abused, within the circle of their own homes, and whose freedom in the South, Mr. Lincoln, as the head of the Republican party, had, as he proclaimed throughout the conflict, sought to avoid, and only consented to its accomplishment when driven to it to save his own race from the dangers and disasters of war.

Slavery throughout the South was abolished, and the present rights of its colored population secured by the adoption of the three late amendments to the Constitution; which could not have been done without the concurrent consent and action of the Southern States. Why should not the colored freemen of the South now greatly prefer to act in political harmony with the Southern white men, who are their real friends, and with whom they are identified in having the same country to live in, and the same interests to protect, rather than to depend upon a sectional party of the North, who have never sought to aid them except for selfish ends and party purposes? In a letter dated Montgomery, Ala., Sept. 20, 1880, from James A. Scott, a colored man, who has been for four years editor of the *Montgomery Advance*, addressed to Col. F. A. Conkling, of New York, brother of Roscoe Conkling, and published in the *New York Sun*, among other things says: "The Republican partisan press is now teeming with abuse against the people of the South, alleging that colored men are 'bull-dozed,' their votes not fairly counted, and their rights and privileges openly denied. Such, sir, is not the fact. Colored men, after calmly and quietly reviewing the events of the last ten years, have very naturally asked themselves, 'What have we gained by our blind adhesion to the Republican party? We have held none of the offices, but on the contrary men have induced us to place them in power, and have grown rich, and left us to our fate; we have received nothing at their hands; we are dependent on the white men of our State for our bread, for our subsistence, for the schooling of our children, for all that we have; we go to them in trouble and distress, and are always treated kindly. They are all in all to us, and why should we oppose them in politics?' Reasoning in this way, the colored men of the South are voting by the hundreds with the white people, and are openly avowing themselves to be Democrats." Why had they not better trust such friends and neighbors, than Northern Republicans, who, as we have seen, have represented their race as "despised" in the North, and where, just eight years before the war, a measure had been enacted so barbarous as the Illinois law of 1853? That act of Mr. Logan, the present Republican leader in Illinois, was founded alone in prejudice against color and race. It did not discriminate the least in favor of the intelligent and upright negro, who had served his state or country in peace or war. Good old Edom London, if he had lived and moved to Illinois, between 1853 and 1865, might have been sold the twelfth time, at auction on the block, under its savage sections. He was an old revolutionary colored soldier, of Massachusetts, who had entered the army of that state, at Cambridge, for eight months. Afterwards he was sold to his tenth master, with whom he lived five weeks, when he enlisted again for three years in the armies of '76. His last owner received all of his bounty, and part of his wages.

In 1806, the old hero became poor, and chargeable to the town in which he resided. That town struggled through all the courts of Massachusetts, from the Justice to the Supreme Court, to shift the responsibility for the scanty support of that old soldier, to one of the numerous towns in which he had sojourned as the slave of eleven masters. In this noted case of Interpleader among the towns of that negro-hating, but professed negro-loving, Republican state of Massachusetts, the burden of supporting this aged veteran of '76, so long shunned and dreaded by the different towns, was at last fastened upon one of them by the decision of the case of *Whichendon Town* v. *Hatfield Town*, reported in 4 Mass. Reports. Edom London was no common character, compared even to the great and good of the earth. His heroism was of the higher life among heroes. Forgetful and careless of the chains he wore himself, he sighed and sought for the liberty of others. He fought on the fields of fame, for no glory to win, no honors to wear, for *himself*. Robbed of his rewards, and of the wages he won, by those for whom he bled, he lived a beggar for his bread, a pauper among a people he had sought to save. In his day of want, there was no well-to-do gentleman in the land of Sumter who would not have pensioned him on sight. But beggared and breadless, as he was made by those whose liberty he had bought with his blood, and shameful as the strife was among the towns to shun his support, we thank God he died in Massachusetts before he reached Illinois, where he might have been sold at auction, on account of the color of his skin, under the law of Mr. Logan, the present Republican Senator from that state, and leader of the Republican party in the Northwest.

Nothing can be more hypocritical and unjustifiable than the effort made by the Republican party since the war to defeat and render odious the Democrats, because they still maintain the old time-honored doctrine of State Rights, as held by Jefferson and Madison. In their platform of 1860, the Republican party adopted the following resolution: "That the maintenance inviolate of the rights of the states, and especially the right of each state to order and control its own domestic institutions according to its own judgment exclusively, is essential to that balance of powers on which the perfection and endurance of our political fabric depends; and we denounce the lawless invasion, by armed force, of the soil of any state or territory, no matter under what pretext, as among the gravest of crimes."

As far as this resolution goes, legitimately construed according to the obvious meaning of its words, it is a partial statement of the true doctrine of state rights, copied from the Democratic records. But it is only a *part* of that doctrine, as will be seen by referring back to our own exposition of it. A most important feature of it is left out of this Republican platform of 1860, which was a party trick, wilfully perpetrated for the accomplishment of an unconstitutional partisan purpose. The feature ignored and condemned by its omission in this platform of 1860, is that the Supreme Court of the Union is to be the final arbiter of the rights of the states and of the General Government, subject only to the ultimate constitutional power of amendment by conventions of the states. This principle, thus omitted, then, *because denied* by the Republican party and its leader, strange to say, is to be found inserted in their platform of 1880, in these words: "Some powers are denied to the nation, while others are denied to the states; but the *boundary* between the powers delegated and those reserved is *to be determined* by the *national*, and not by the state *tribunals*." The reason of this is, that in 1860 the Supreme Court had decided an important question against the opinion of that party, and, therefore, its authority was denied. *Now*, the court has a majority of Republicans, made so by the *party* act of increasing the number of the judges, in order that the majority might manufacture opinions, as they have done, to order; and, *therefore*, the authority of the court is recognized in their platform of 1880. Before the Republican party obtained possession of the Federal Government, they not only advocated all the existing constitutional rights of the states, but claimed and exercised many others which were unconstitutional and did not exist. Since they have acquired federal power, they have reversed their policy. Now they have not only abandoned their claim for illegitimate state sovereignty, which they had so long exercised, but striking from their platform of 1880 the resolution for constitutional State Rights, which they had borrowed from the Democratic party, and inserted in its place, not only that judicial federal authority which in 1860 they denied, but claims for Federal power unauthorized by the Constitution.

The Republican party, before the war, was organized and

trained in a school hostile to the Federal Government. Its state legislators commenced their work, as has been seen, by the advocacy and passage of "Personal Liberty bills," to defeat the enforcement by the Federal Government of a plain constitutional provision, which each one had taken a solemn oath to support. A specimen of these has been given in citing the rebellious and nullifying act of Vermont. Others of a like kind might have been cited, such as the act of Massachusetts, which provided penalties and imprisonment, against her own citizens, for aiding in the execution of that same clause of the federal Constitution. Another instance has been given where the Republican party in Ohio, through their distinguished leader, Gov. Chase, in 1857, pledged the whole power of that state to resist the process of the Federal court. Another, is the abrogation and disregard, by that party, of the decision of the Supreme Court, rendered in the Dred Scott case in 1857. The following resolution was passed by the Legislature of Wisconsin, in 1859, the Republican members unanimously voting for it: "Resolved, That the principle and construction contended for by the party which now rules in the councils of the nation (*i. e.* the Democratic party), that the General Government is the exclusive judge of the extent of the powers delegated to it, stop nothing short of despotism, since the discretion of those who administer the government, and not the Constitution, would be the measure of their powers; that the several states which framed that instrument, being sovereign and independent, have the unquestionable right to judge of its infractions, and that a *positive defiance* of the sovereignties of all unauthorized acts done, or attempted to be done, under color of that instrument, is the rightful remedy." The Democrats in the Wisconsin Legislature, of course, *unanimously* voted against this resolution; as *no such* had ever been adopted by their party; nor was it like, either in letter or spirit, the Virginia proceedings of 1798–99, which we have reviewed; but under a profession of state rights and state sovereignty, the above resolution, adopted with entire unanimity by the Republican party in Wisconsin, was treasonable and rebellious against the Federal Government. This resolution stood undisturbed until 1863, when the following repealing act was passed by the Wisconsin Legislature: "That joint resolutions No. 4, adopted by the Legislature in 1859, being substantially the same as the Kentucky resolutions of 1798, which have been endorsed by the

Democratic party in national and state conventions, and explained and construed in aid of secession and rebellion, in the opinion of this Legislature, ought to be, and the same are hereby, disavowed and rescinded." The Democrats, of course, voted against such a repealing act, because its statement that the Wisconsin and Kentucky resolutions were substantially the same, was *false*, and its imputation against their party was a *slander*. So it was passed alone by Republican votes. Before this repeal, during the election contests of 1859-60, the Republicans used these treasonable resolutions in a spirit of "*defiance*" against the Federal Government, and as the states rights' doctrine of their party. After, however, they came into possession of that Government, and commenced their career of centralization, the order came in 1863 for their repeal, and so these, like the resolution of 1860, which has been noticed, are also omitted in the Republican platforms of 1880.

Mr. Wade, the Republican Senator of Ohio, afterwards the Republican Vice President, in the Senate of the United States, uttered these words: "Who is to be the judge, in the last resort, of the violations of the Constitution of the United States by the enactment of a law? Who, sir, is the final arbiter? The General Government, or the states in their sovereignty? Why, sir, to yield that point, is to yield up all the rights of the states to protect their citizens, and to consolidate this Government into a miserable despotism. I tell you, sir, whatever you may think of it, if this bill pass, collisions will arise between the federal and state jurisdictions, conflicts more dangerous than all the wordy wars which are got up in Congress; conflicts in which the states will never yield. My state believed it unconstitutional, and that under the old resolutions of 1798 and 1799 *a state* must not only be the judge of that, but of the remedy in such a case." Here, again, we see that misconstruction of the resolutions of 1798, which we have heretofore noticed, and that treasonable heresy proclaimed and supported by the Republicans *before the war*, that a *single state* has the right to judge of the unconstitutionality of an act of Congress, and of the mode and measure of redress." It was shortly after these utterances that Mr. Chase, the Republican Governor of Ohio, gave an order to enforce this doctrine of state resistance against the General Government, to which we have referred, all proving a concert of action between the most distinguished leaders of the Republican party, in advocating and practicing a state sovereignty wholly unknown to the Constitution. In the presence of such a record, how false to truth—how lost to all shame—must be the Republican, who can denounce a Democrat as a disunionist for maintaining the reserved rights of the states and the union of the Constitution, as defined by Jefferson and Madison in the resolutions of 1798; a union which Republicans but yesterday sought to sever,—rights which they seek to-day to destroy.

In their effort to centralize and consolidate the Government, the Republicans contend, that the war was a decision against the Democratic doctrine of State Rights. The equivalent of such a declaration is, that it was the destruction of the Government itself, which is an absurdity. We have stated the principles assumed by the Republican party which resulted in the conflict between the South and the North. For their reunion, the North fought the South, and for that alone, as proclaimed over and over again from the beginning to the end of the war. Those principles were briefly:

1st. The avowed refusal of the Republican party, on coming into power, to allow the Southerners to go into any of the common territories of the United States with their slave property, and to regard the decision of the Supreme Court in favor of their constitutional right to do so, as the law of the land until reversed, and, as such, binding on all the departments of the Government.

2d. The avowed refusal of the Republican party to allow the fugitive slave clause of the Constitution to be executed.

These conclusions, therefore, necessarily follow:

First. The war decided that the grounds on which the South acted were not sufficient to authorize a separation.

Secondly. That an attempted separation on such grounds was cause for war to reunite the two sections.

The peaceful results which followed after the close of the war, by the consent of the Southern states, under the pressure of circumstances, were the three amendments to the Constitution, which have been noticed. By one of these, slavery was abolished; which being the only subject on which the constitutional questions producing the war were based, those questions can never again arise, nor can their settlement form a precedent for the settlement of *other* issues having no relation whatever to slavery.

Before leaving this subject of the war, let us recall to mind a few significant and weighty words, uttered in the midst of its closing scenes, by him who had the right to speak, as the oracle of his party. Mr. Lincoln said: "Slavery had in some way been the cause of the war." "He believed the people of the North were as responsible for slavery as the people of the South." On another occasion he said: "If we shall suppose that American slavery is one of those offenses which in the Providence of God must needs come, but which having continued through His appointed time, He now wills to remove, and that He gives to both North and South this terrible war as the woe due to those by whom the offense came, shall we discover therein any departure from those divine attributes which the believers in a living God always ascribe to him?" It is said by those nearest him and who knew him best, that at this time Mr. Lincoln had a presentiment of his death, then near at hand. Under the solemnities of such a premonition, and of his second Presidential oath fresh upon his lips, he proclaimed it as a truth, of which he had the profoundest conviction, that for all the wrongs of American slavery, the North and South were *equally guilty;* and addressing himself to the former, said: "And to you of the *North*, triumphant over the South, I say, '*Judge not that ye be not judged.*'" The application of the precept from Holy Writ *was as true* as the precept itself was divine. The utter desecration of it by the Republican party of the North, in their vilification of the South, has been as marked as was the blasphemy of the Scribes and Pharisees against Him who gave it!

www.ingramcontent.com/pod-product-compliance
Lightning Source LLC
Chambersburg PA
CBHW031605110426
42742CB00037B/1264